BOWLAND & THE SOUTH PE

A Hillwalkers' Companion

WYCOLLER

Cataloguing in Publication Data

Gillham, John 1947-
Bowland & the South Pennines: A Hillwalkers' Companion.
1.   Lancashire, Forest of Bowland
      – Visitors's Guides
2.   England, South Pennines – Visitors Guides
I.   Title.
      914.2768504859
      914.281
ISBN 0-9515996-0-7

JOHN GILLHAM was born in 1947 in Bournemouth. He has lived in Lancashire for most of his life, building up a detailed knowledge of the Pennine Hills. After many years at British Aerospace, he is now a full time writer/photogrpaher and publisher.

PHIL IDDON was born in Chorley in 1954. He has a degree in Mechanical Engineering and works as a senior engineer with British Aeorospace at Preston. He began mountain walking in 1977 and particularly likes the French Alps and Scottish Mountains. He is married and lives in the Ribble Valley beneath the shadow of Pendle Hill.

ACKNOWLEDGMENTS: I would like to thank those who have helped me in the publication of this book. My friend Phil Iddon has done a marvellous job writing and describing Pendle. In our next book about the Dales he will take a major role, which his photography merits. Those who have been good companions to me on the Fells include, Phil, his wife, Sheila, my niece Sherril Clayton and last but definitely not least, my wife, Nicola who has also been very supportive throughout. Ken Wilson, this country's best mountain book producer, has been very patient in giving advice on the publishing side, as has Ken Vickers of Cordee.

All photographs by John Gillham except those on Pendle Hill which have been taken by Phil Iddon. All maps and other line illustrations are by John Gillham.

Front Cover Photo: Ward's Stone Plateau looking eastwards to Ingleborough & Whernside.

I would like to dedicate this book to my wife, Nicola and also to my mum and dad

ALSO BY THE SAME AUTHOR:–
"Snowdonia to the Gower"   Diadem Books

BOWLAND & THE SOUTH PENNINES

A Hillwalkers' Companion

by

John Gillham

with section on Pendle Hill written and
photographed by Phil Iddon.

GREY STONE BOOKS
Hoddlesden

CONTENTS

INTRODUCTION

The hills of Bowland and Pendle face those of the South Pennines from opposite sides of the industrial East Lancashire Plains. Aesthetically they are poles apart and, until one studies the map, may seem strange bedfellows to include within one book. The South Pennines, though not without natural beauty, have been savaged and scarred by the industries of yesteryear whilst Bowland is largely untainted and completely rural. The contrasts are complimentary however, and both will appeal to the walker who likes his hills uncrowded and quiet. Most of the South Pennine scars are healing. The quarries are being enveloped by grass and mosses, the reservoir shores have mellowed into their environment and the sound of machinery has been replaced by that of rustling breezes and birdsong.

The Forest of Bowland has, quite rightly, been specified under the National Parks Act as an 'Area of Outstanding Natural Beauty' and covers an expanse of three hundred square miles, mainly of high gritstone, heather-clad moors of the Pennine genre. Many of Bowland's sightseers are town dwellers from Central Lancashire and the Fylde Coast. Few stray far from their automobiles, choosing instead to congregate in road-side honey-pots. This is a shame, for they are so remote from the region's true character - a character which can be as meek as the lambs that play in its meadows ; as sweet as the birdsong that echoes in the silence of its moors and as mellow as the morning sunshine that dances in breeze-blown hillside grasses and purple heather. And yet in contrast it can throw out a challenge to rugged mountain walkers and be as harsh as the icy winds that thrash and erode the high tops. It can possess a disposition as dark and unyielding as the millstone grit crags that crest its peaks and as vigorous as the waters that cascade in its cloughs.

My first fell walk in Bowland involved a short expedition to the top of Whins Brow near the high pass known as the Trough of Bowland. It was a grey, lifeless January day but the journey did leave me with a desire to return. I set myself a target in true peak-bagging style, making a list of all those hills whose height exceeded fifteen hundred feet which I then systematically scaled.

My affinity with Bowland's hills became more than mathematical and, although this harsh mistress more often than not left me with my boots and socks caked with gooey peat and my clothes waterlogged, we attained an amicable friendship and understanding. Often through a shroud of pale clinging mist, I discovered her secret cloughs and hidden cascades - those quiet places known by few save the curlews, plovers or grouse. I explored the long valleys that are riven deep into the hills' secluded heartlands far beyond the civilisation of the last isolated farm-houses. These valleys provide some of the finest walking routes where the serenity and quietude is seldom equalled. One old pack-horse route, the Hornby Road (sometimes known as the Salters' Fell Track)

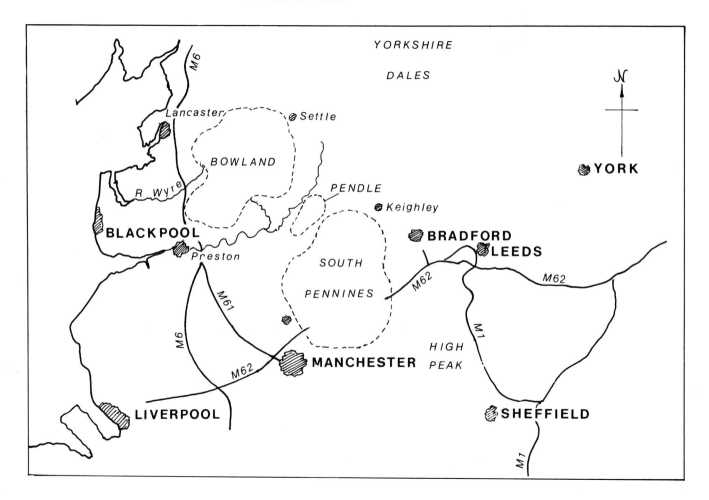

passes the heads of three such valleys, Croasdale, Whitendale and Roeburndale. It has been described as the finest moorland walk in Britain-certainly it is one of the best offerings on England's northern fells.

As much as I love Bowland, certain aspects of the local democracy fill me with ire. Major land-owners try to keep the highlands private for their exclusive use as grouse-shooting moors. I am one of a growing band of people who believe that the high fells should be open for all to freely roam providing that due respect for the environment and wild life is exercised. The Lancashire County Council have, to their credit, negotiated a few courtesy paths to Fair Snape and Ward's Stone but STILL OUT OF BOUNDS after agreements were White Hill (1784ft); Wolfhole Crag (1731ft); Totridge Fell (1621ft); Great Harlow (1595ft); Hawthornthwaite Fell Top (1568ft); Whins Brow (1565ft); and Baxton Fell (1534ft). ALL are of considerable interest to the hillwalker and ALL have their very special character. In addition, certain restrictions were added to the agreement at the owners' request, mainly to accommodate the grouse shooting fraternity. The routes would be closed on August 12th (the start of the grouse season) and on up to ten additional days to the end of the season on December 12th. No dogs were to be allowed, no fires to be lit, and camping would be prohibited

Tales of witchcraft have for a long time contributed to the mystique of Pendle Hill following the famous trials at Lancaster where, in 1612, nineteen poor souls were found guilty and cruelly hanged. On a sunless day Pendle's escarpment truly assumes its satanic role, rising dark and sullenly from the surrounding pastures. Halloween is celebrated annually hereabouts by locals who undertake a candlelit procession to Pendle's summit.

Villages within the region are picturesque and full of character, especially Chipping, Slaidburn and Downham, and they all wait to serve the needs of the leg-weary traveller. It is quite a tonic ,on descending the hills, to enjoy a 'contemplative' pint at one of the fine old inns.

*   *   *

The South Pennines are harsh moors with a core of dark millstone grit which often surfaces in strangely eroded boulders. The impervious nature of this rock and its ability to retain water make the South Pennines ideal for the construction of reservoirs and there are hundreds from the smallest, built to supply the quarries and mines, to the more modern, which supplied the ever-growing demands of the towns following industrial revolution.

Few South Pennine peaks are truly remote for they are parcelled by high moorland roads and glaciated steep-sided sylvan deans. Deep cloughs descend from the bare moors, cut by rushing streams which are then cleansed to purity by their thrashing on hard rock beds. It is the number and purity of these streams which gave birth to the weaving mills and, since the industrial revolution, the valleys have been home to the pioneers of mining, spinning and weaving. The tremendous hardship that followed is reflected in the austerity of the architecture, but somehow these harsh 'prisons' have mellowed into quaintness and merged into their surroundings as if they had always been there.

The towns have grown up around the mills and beside them are railways, roads and canals. Relics of earlier industries are often found on the hills - the ancient mines and quarries, which have for decades been derelict and have returned almost to the fellsides, and also ancient highways which straddle high moors often paved with slabs of millstone grit. The finest is the Blackstone Edge road, which is said to have been of Roman origin although the present paving is more likely to date back to medieval times. These roads and causeways make excellent paths and take the walker back to the times when pack-horses would have struggled along them conveying such cargo as lime, coal and salt to the town markets.

I have, since starting the book, come to live in the Pennine village of Hoddlesden and feel I can proudly say that these are the hills of home. They are definitely not the most picturesque, the most majestic or the best conserved hills (far from it), but they have a sense of drama and history not evident elsewhere.

North West Water are major landowners in both Bowland and the South Pennines. After privatisation, there is uncertainty in the long term over the access agreements on their domain. I can only hope that the pressure groups like the Ramblers' Association keep up their constant vigil on the situation.

The walks I have include in the book are biased towards the high moors and are directed at the experienced fellwalker.

Whitendale

None of them are too demanding for an averagely fit person ,but the knowledge of how to use a map and compass is essential for, as with all high fells, bad weather and low cloud can turn a leisurely stroll into a dangerous nightmare. My sketches are in no way intended to substitute for proper Ordnance Survey maps. At the start of each walk I have related the relevant maps-both 1:50000 Landranger and 1:25000 (larger scale) Outdoor Leisure Maps. The latter are strongly recommended for South Pennine routes which tend to cross complex farm pastures before striking for the hills. (the Landranger series do not mark the position of field boundaries or name many farms or streams, essential for following routes through farmland.)

MOUNTAINS	HEIGHT(feet)	AREA	ROUTE
Ward's Stone	1836	Bowland	4,5
Pendle Hill	1831	"	12-15
White Hill*	1784	"	-
Wolfhole Crag*	1731	"	-
Fair Snape Fell	1707	"	6-9
Boulsworth Hill	1699	South Pennines	26-27
Totridge Fell*	1629	Bowland	-
Great Harlow*	1595	"	-
Black Hameldon	1575	South Pennines	29-31
Hawthornthwaite Fell*	1568	Bowland	-
Whins Brow	1565	"	11
Blackstone Edge	1548	South Pennines	16,17
Grit Fell	1531	Bowland	5
Withins Height	1505	South Pennines	28
High Brown Knoll	1489	" "	22
Inchfield Moor	1488	" "	24
Thieveley Beacon	1473	" "	25
Wolf Stones	1455	" "	32,33
Rough Hill	1423	" "	24
Hades Hill	1419	" "	24
Parlick	1416	Bowland	8
Clougha Pike	1350	"	1-3
Stoodley Pike	1330	South Pennines	18-21

* There are no rights of way or access agreements to these summits

THE BOWLAND HILLS

The Forest of Bowland, which is largely in Lancashire, includes a group of high heather-clad, peaty hills encircled by the towns of Preston, Lancaster and Settle. These hills decline to the valleys of the Lune, Wenning, Ribble and also a more artificial twentieth century border, the M6 motorway.

The word 'forest' in Bowland's title refers not to the modern translation but is derived from 'foris', which meant "land only fit for game hunting". It was the Norman baron, Robert de Lacey who declared Bowland a Royal Forest and ,in the centuries that followed, the prolific Red and Fallow deer were hunted to their extinction within the area. (The last one was recorded in 1805) Today the Sika and Roe deer can be sited here.

The area was, however expansively covered with deciduous woodlands until cleared by those lowland farmers, the Angles. In medieval times, when most of today's cattle farms were established, the lowlands were cleared on a much larger scale. A multitude of small broad-leafed woodland copses still exist amidst low farmlands but today a new type of forest is being planted. Regimented legions of fast-growing dark-leafed conifers, notably that American import, the Sitka Spruce, blanket large areas by the Stocks Reservoir and in the Dunsop Valley. I can only hope their march will be more controlled than those swelling battalions of Scotland and Wales!

Some of the oldest evidence of settlement within this most sparsely populated area include the old bronze age circle at Bleasdale, and the Roman road linking Ribchester and Burrow. This scales Longridge Fell before continuing over Salter Fell from Newton.

Bowland's highest hill is Ward's Stone at 1836ft. This gritstone capped moor is probably the most popular, followed by its lower outlier Clougha Pike and Fair Snape Fell to the south of the region.

Three lovely rivers have cut wide and verdant valleys between Bowland's heather-clad hillsides. These are the Wyre, which has its source on the Ward's Stone ridge, the Hodder and the Calder. Tributaries such as Langden Brook, and the Dunsop, Brennand and Whitendale Rivers flow in wilder valleys deep into the bare inner moorlands.

The amount of walks available have been limited by the few rights of way and scant access available on the high fells. Many hills that I would like to have included are alas out of bounds unless you are a fee-paying grouse shooter. There are many natural routes that I would have liked to have seen 'legalised' such as the high northern ridge walk between

White Moss and Hawthornthwaite Fell Top.

Looking on the positive side however, those who complete the fifteen walks I have included will have seen some of Bowland's finest features.

Clougha Pike in the west near Lancaster and Black Hill in the east near Settle. This would traverse twenty miles of some of England's wildest moorland including the summits of Ward's Stone, Wolfhole Crag and White Hill, Bowland's three highest fells. Another good but tough walk would have been a Langden Brook 'Horseshoe' taking in Totridge, Fair Snape,

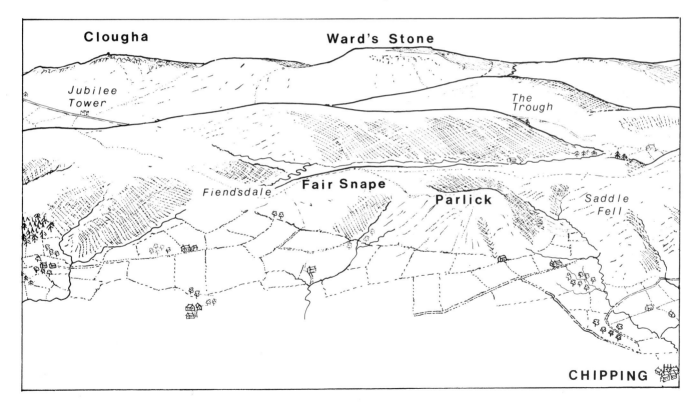

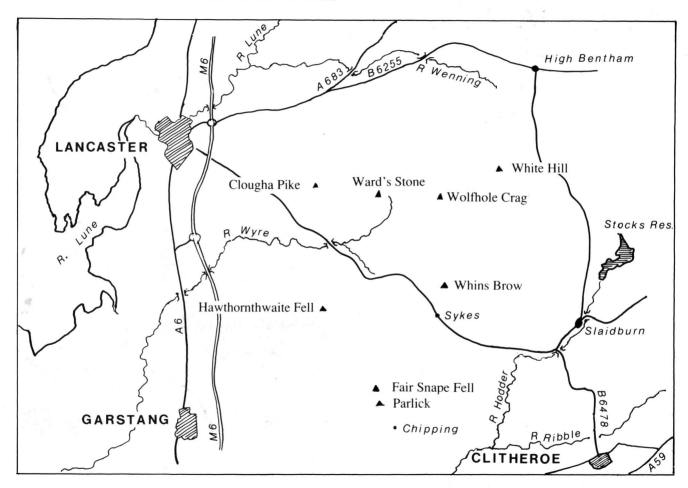

CLOUGHA PIKE

O.S. Landranger Maps 1;50000 Nos 102 & 97

Route 1 From Quernmore (Rigg Lane Car Park)
Route 2 From the Jubilee Tower
Route 3 From Quernmore Village via Routen Brook

At little over thirteen hundred feet Clougha Pike, pronounced Cloffa, is fairly low in the Bowland league of heights. In my opinion however, it is at the top of the list for aesthetic appeal and interest- a veritable playground for walkers, scramblers, students of botany, geology and fell-runners alike.

It is a rocky peak in miniature amongst an area of loftier undulating moorland and yet, when viewed from the east ,it becomes evident that Clougha is but the bony knuckle of Ward's Stone's long heather-clad arm.

The fell's eastern bastion, Birk Bank projects boldly from peaceful pastures that surround the tiny hamlet of Quernmore (pronounced Quarmer). The oakwood cover on its lower slopes hide the barren gritstone surface in all but the winter months, but the concealment ends beyond Windy Clough, where the splintered cliffs known as Clough Scar, rise in three 'steps' to the summit of the Pike.

The northern fellsides are thickly laden with heather and their concave slopes are more featureless and thus of little interest to the hiker. To the south of the summit, Hare Apple-tree Fell, a wet coarse grassland, descends to a high country lane near to the Jubilee Tower, whilst, to the east the heathery

On the summit of Clougha

ridge swells, scarred with a myriad peat hags to the heights of Grit Fell and beyond to Ward's Stone.

To reach the summit of Clougha Pike demands little of the seasoned walker in terms of time or energy used. Often it is the first stop on an itinerary which includes Ward's Stone - one that I cannot recommend for you sip a good wine and so you should amble up Clougha, less mindful of the constraints of passing time. If you want to introduce your offsprings to the delights of fellwalking , here is a good place.

In vast vistas, the Lancashire and Cumbria coastline can be traced noting landmarks including Blackpool Tower, Heysham Power Station and, across the sands of Morecambe Bay, the town of Barrow. Those connoisseurs of Lakeland will be able to pick out the outlines of its mountains from the rounded Black Combe in the west to the High Street Range in the east. If the gaze is diverted towards Yorkshire, the shapely limestone mountains of Ingleborough Whernside and Pen-y-Ghent dominate the landscape beyond the Ribble Valley.

ROUTE 1
CLOUGHA PIKE from the Rigg Lane Car Park, Quernmore

Distance 2 miles (one way) -easy

This short walk must rank as one of the finest in Bowland and, if undertaken on a fine clear Autumn afternoon, the conditions will be at their most enhancing with the western sunshine highlighting Clougha's gritstone flanks and exag-gerating the russet hues of the oakwoods en route.

The walk commences beyond a stile to the rear of Rigg Lane Car Park (ref. 526605) where a wide track leads east-wards with the craggy wooded flanks of Birk Bank directly ahead. After fifty yards a right fork in the tracks is taken. This descends to a five-bar gate marked 'strictly Private' which is a shame because beyond lies a beautifully situated tree-enshrouded lake. The way, however is to the left over a wooden stile. The field on the other side is marshy and the path is constructed of duck-boards for much of the way to the next stile at its far edge. From here the going improves and the path wends around gorse bushes and then through a copse of wondrously twisted sessile oak. A small but boisterous brook rushes noisily by on the right hand side whilst ahead the dark crags of Windy Clough are increasingly revealed.

Two stiles are handily placed at the intersection of tall dry-stone walls at the foot of Windy Clough. The succeeding paths both eventually lead to the summit of Clougha Pike but, for the most interesting route, use the one on the left, then turn right to climb across marshy grasslands close to the line of the wall towards the ridge. Physical traces of the path disappear amongst rough slopes of rock, heather, and bilberry inter-spersed with more wind-stunted oaks. Near to the top of the ridge is a fine example of a mountain spring. Its position can be recognised from afar by its surround of vivid green mosses and lush grass.

On reaching the ridge, a wall is followed. Clougha's sleek slopes of shattered gritstone rise magnificently from the

Looking across Morecambe Bay from Clougha

Approaching Long Crag, Ward's Stone from Tarnbrook

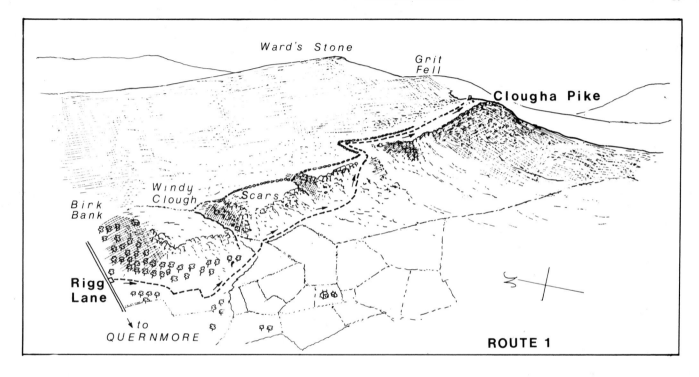

Ward's Stone

Grit Fell

Clougha Pike

Windy
Clough

Scars

Birk
Bank

**Rigg
Lane**

↓ to
QUERNMORE

ROUTE 1

colourful moorland shelf and the now distinct path amongst firmer peat, heather and huge boulders is a joy to walk. The extensive views to Ribblesdale and Morecambe Bay double the pleasure!

Clougha's summit is a gem! It is crowned with rock, complete with the customary stone shelter and concrete trig-point and gives marvellous views of the Three peaks of Yorkshire and many of the famous Lakeland mountains. For those whose eyes are drawn to Ward's Stone, Clougha's lofty neighbour , do not be tempted to make the journey. The peat-hagged heathery terrain which lies between is dull and you will not see the best of Bowland's highest hill.

Route 2
CLOUGHA PIKE from the Jubilee Tower

Distance 1¹/₂ miles (one way) - fairly easy

The shortest route to Clough's summit involves just four-hundred feet of ascent and starts at Jubilee Tower, (ref. 543573). It is not a spectacular approach but perhaps ideal for a summer evening walk - one to view the spectacular sunsets over Morecambe Bay. At this time of year the fiery skies would be a back-drop to the Lake District's shapely peaks!

From the Tower's car park , take a bearing of 5° (North) with Clougha's craggy crest directly ahead rising above the long golden grasses of Hare Appletree Fell. The way is trackless, initially - the first landmark is a tall wooden post. From here it is easy to see, on the horizon ,the stile which must be located to cross the barbed-wire fence barring the way to our objective. From the stile, Clougha Pike stands proudly, displaying more clearly its rugged southern face beyond Rowten Brook which is little more than a trickle at this altitude.

The path becomes increasingly obvious as Clougha is approached and joins a path from Routen Brook Farm, just preceding the final pull on a rocky ramp to the summit.

Alternative Start.

There is room for a couple of cars to park at ref. 534582 opposite to a small stand of larch trees close to Hare Appletree Farm.

The stream, known as Damas Gill, is followed , and then crossed to the left hand banks when its grassy ravine becomes more shallow. The route meets that from Jubilee Tower by the previously mentioned wooden post.

Jubilee Tower

ROUTE 3
CLOUGHA PIKE From Quernmore via Rowten Brook

Distance 2 miles (one way)- easy.

Another short,easy walk to Clougha Pike starts at the crossroads just to the east of Quernmore's village centre (ref. 520590).

Clougha Pike

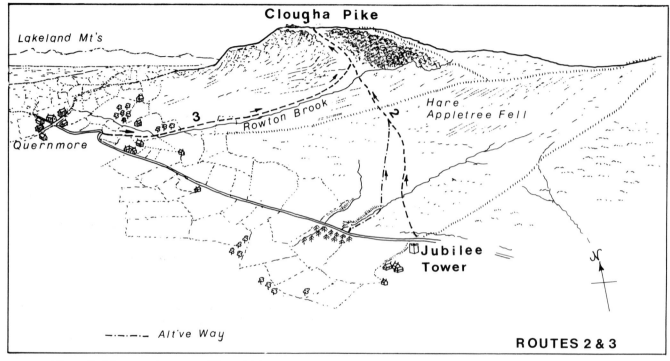

Clougha Pike

Lakeland Mt's

Rowton Brook

Hare
Appletree Fell

3

2

Quernmore

Jubilee
Tower

N

— · — · — Alt've Way

ROUTES 2 & 3

After climbing up the steep 'Trough' lane an east-bound track from ref. 523590 is followed , taking the left fork a short while later. This reaches Routen Brook Farm where a well used path continues across fields and to the south of a wood.

The path keeps to the south of Rowten Brook until ,on the open fellsides, it crosses to assume a north easterly direction with Clougha Pike's crags and outcrops boldly rising from the moorland spread. The final climb rakes across these crags using the same rocky shelf as the Jubilee Tower route. It would perhaps be a good idea to return via the Rigg Lane car park (route 1) and follow the minor road back to the village.

WARD'S STONE

O.S. Landranger Map 1:50000 No.102

Route 4 From Tower Lodge, Abbeystead
Route 5 From the Jubilee Tower

Bowland's highest hill can boast no distinctive profiles or rocky buttresses and, rising from an already lofty moorland platform, does not give an accurate impression of its elevation. It forms part of a ridge which spans between Clougha Pike to the west and Burn Moor to the east. The real attraction of Ward's Stone lies in the wide panoramas of Morecambe Bay, the Lakeland Fells and the peaks of Yorkshire.

Tarnbrook Fell, the southern facade, is also its fairest. Here the infant River Wyre has gouged a fine valley from the dark beds of millstone grit that form the tops of these hills. The concave heather-clad slopes to the west of the river are crested by splintered bouldery cliffs known as Long Crag which form the southern edge of the summit plateau. The plateau undulates and swells in a vast tract of peat haggs and heather to the highest land marked by two concrete trig. points, separated by a third of a mile. The most visited summit is the western one and is recognised by the huge boulder known as Ward's Stone. The eastern neighbour has a couple of boulders known as the Grey Mare and Foal, which are squat and not so impressive.

Ward's Stone's eastern slopes decline to Mallowdale Fell, whose pointed Pike defiantly stands sentry high above the beautiful sylvan valley of Roeburndale. In the north the Foxdale and Uldale Becks have carved their niches in the barren hills before descending to the picturesque Littledale.

There are no rights of way to Ward's Stone and all routes on higher ground are on negotiated access strips with all the restrictions which that entails. (see introduction)

ROUTE 4
WARD'S STONE from Tower Lodge, Abbeystead

Distance 7¹/₂ miles (one way)- hard- difficult in mist.

This unusual route to Ward's Stone involves an extra five hundred feet of ascent and adds three miles to the more traditional 'Tarnbrook' way. For this I make no apology and, if a fine day is chosen for the trip, none will be required. The views from the top of White Moor over the valley of the Tarnbrook Wyre towards Ward's Stone are more than compensation for the additional efforts .

There is space for a few cars near to the Tower Lodge (ref 604539) at the start of the walk. This ivy-clad dwelling stands in a shallow vale between the barren fellsides of Blaze Moss and White Moor. The spartan surroundings are allevi-

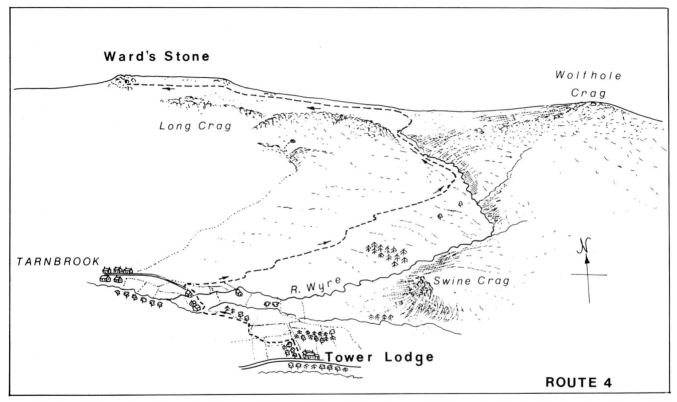

ROUTE 4

ated by the tall Scots Pines lining the Marshaw Wyre, which flows close to the road.

The northbound track by the side of the lodge has mixed woodland to the left and climbs towards White Moor.

When the open fell is reached the track is abandoned for a right of way which is not obvious underfoot. A bearing of 290° will set the coarse for the first of four stiles. The path is easy from here as each stile is visible from its neighbour and the paths across moorland become less sketchy. A stone wall , close to the highest point of White Moor, is scaled using primitive built-in steps. It is from here that the view of Ward's Stone's southern face (Tarnbrook Fell) is seen at its finest. Beyond the stone buildings of Speight Clough Farm and Gilberton just

Tower Lodge

below, the cart track to be used on the ascent can be traced meandering up the fellside to the splintered gritstone scars known as Long Crag. The River Tarnbrook Wyre, which separates White Moor from Ward's Stone, is surrounded by pastures, parcelled into intricate patchwork patterns by dry-stone walls which have stood for so many generations. As the distant track veers northwards below Swine Crag, it enters an

expansive uncluttered landscape of rough heathland.

After passing through the yard of Speight Clough, head for Gilberton Farm where a wooden footbridge spanning the Tarnbrook Wyre leads to a narrow metalled lane. This, in turn, leads to the Ward's Stone track, sighted earlier. A right turn is made along the stony track which climbs steadily up Tarnbrook Fell. It terminates at a ruined shelter which over-looks the infant Wyre, rushing and splashing amongst the dark boulders by which it is enclosed. The retrospective view over the Wyre's craggy clough towards Hawthornthwaite Fell and the Trough of Bowland is worthy of note at this point.

The river is crossed just beyond some diminutive waterfalls and the journey continues on a well defined track to the ridge fence (ref. 618583). Views across Ribblesdale to the Three Peaks will dominate the senses if the atmospheric conditions allow. The track along the ridge appears circuitous but do not be tempted to make a beeline for the summit of Ward's Stone ,for the horrible peat hags and ankle twisting heathery terrain will make the going very rough indeed. The bare peat found in places on the correct route is sticky in parts but rarely is it troublesome.

The fence ends a couple of hundred yards short of the eastern summit of Ward's Stone doubling back acutely and descending Mallowdale Fell. This eastern summit is seldom visited although of a similar elevation to its neighbour. The rocks which mark it are known as the Grey Mare and Foal. I have studied their outlines from each angle but alas, I have to say that my imagination must be more restricted than the

On the Summit of Ward's Stone

fellow who Christened this natural monument for I can see no resemblance.

The more famous western summit , which houses the huge boulder from which the hill took its name, is about a third of a mile distant over fairly firm ground. It is worth visiting for its superior vistas of Morecambe Bay and the Lake District peaks. There is no form of shelter on the summits but various crevices in the boulders will provide adequate protection from the elements.

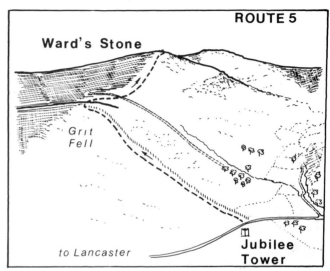

ROUTE 5
WARD'S STONE from the Jubilee Tower

Distance 4 miles (one way)-moderate to hard -difficult in mist.

Although the quickest way to the summit and one of the most popular, this is the least interesting and more suited to those with little time available or to fell runners, whose heads are usually bowed towards the ground underfoot.

A fence leading from the ample car-park north-east-wards to the skyline, is followed across dull moorlands, whose terrain is squelchy and thick with rough grass and mosses. On the high ridge is a huge stone cairn known as the Shooters' Pile. To the left of the fence is common land whilst to its right are the carefully nurtured heathlands that are the strictly private Tarnbrook Grouse Moors.

Shortly after passing the Shooters' Pile the ridge is attained just to the west of Grit Fell's summit. A stile on the right enables the fence to be crossed and a well cairned easterly course made over Grit Fell. Ward's Stone can be clearly seen beyond a slight depression in the vast tract of heather lying between. A wide flinted cart track, not visible from afar, is crossed at the base of the depression. Markers lay down the extent of the allowed access strip hereabouts reminding us that these hills are not free. After the bland moorland traversed on the subsequent ascent, the gritstone boulders which decorate the higher slopes of Ward's Stone make a welcome change and the new panoramas revealed of Yorkshire's peaks from the summit offer true compensation.

The western summit of Fair Snape

FAIR SNAPE FELL & PARLICK

O.S. Landranger Map 1:50000 No.102

Route 6 From Langden Castle
Route 7 From Saddle End
Route 8 From Fell Foot
Route 9 From Bleasdale Post Office

Fair Snape Fell is the highest peak in a high horse-shoe ridge of hills which surround Langden Brook to the west of Dunsop Bridge. Situated at the south-western tip of the group, it rises gracefully from the green fields of Bleasdale in steep grassy slopes. In its skyline profile from the west it appears as a huge whaleback with Parlick ,its southern outlier, taking the form of its prominent tail.

Like Ward's Stone, Fair Snape has two summits. The more popular one 1675ft high lies on firm ground at the fell's western edge and yields superb far reaching views over the flatlands of the Fylde to Blackpool Tower and further northwards to the Lakeland Peaks which lie across Morecambe Bay. It has all the furniture associated with true summits - a large stone shelter, trig. point and a huge cairn with resident pole (Paddy's Pole). However it is not the true summit which lies half a mile to the north east amidst a morass of sticky peat, partially covered by sphagnum moss and heather. A modest pile of stones mark the spot,which is 1707ft above sea level.

To the north, the peat-hagged plateau descends to Webster's Meadow at the edges of Bleasdale and Fiendsdale. Here the heathered slopes, now drier, plummet to the bouldery edges of their respective streams which flow into Langden Brook.

Fair Snape's southern ridge is grassy and less rough. After descending and narrowing to Nick's Chair, said by the superstitious and more romantic to be a favourite of the Devil himself, it rises to Parlick.

Parlick is one of the most visited high places in Bowland. The track from Fell Foot is now showing terrible scars of erosion from the processions of fellwalkers, sightseers and hang-gliding enthusiasts (the soaring currents of Blindhurst and Fair Snape make Parlick an ideal springboard for this sport). Fortunately from all other angles the hill is untainted , its unrelenting steep ,grassy flanks soaring to the skyline as God intended.

ROUTE 6
FAIR SNAPE FELL from Langden Castle

Distance - 6¹/₂ miles (one way)- very hard

This long valley approach to Fair Snape Fell begins south of Sykes Farm at the map ref 633513. Here a conifer-lined lane leads to the Langden Intake Water Works, whose castellated towers have confused enough tourists to warrant a sign officially stating that this was NOT Langden Castle, which was further on and "not a castle anyway".

From the water works a stony cart track continues on the north side of the Langden Brook, a shallow watercourse flowing along a wide bouldered bed which suggests that the area has been troubled by extensive flooding at some time. Oak and mountain ash decorate more sheltered spots on the

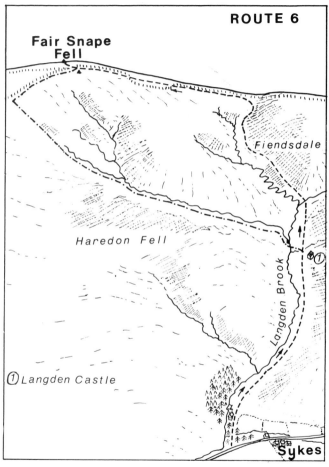

Langden Castle

early stages of the trek but these thin out as the landscape becomes more untamed and the steep bare slopes of Holdren

Moss and Haredon Fell close in on the now reed-ridden river basin.

At the confluence with Bleadale Water, Langden Brook widens. A cobbled section of the track descends to a lush green oasis that surrounds Langden Castle, which turns out to be no more than a stone-built, tin-roofed shepherd's hut. It is now much frequented by both sheep and fell walkers who require shelter from hostile weather.

Beyond the castle, the footpath diverges from the track. It is marked by yellow tipped posts and descends to the river passing through an area of bracken. The fording of the river, which must be made just before the confluence with Fiendsdale Water, is difficult after heavy rains but never is it treacherous.

On the opposite banks, a narrow path rises on heathered slopes and southwards out of the Langden Valley. Below, Fiendsdale's stream meanders in a very regular fashion and assumes the appearance of a glistening serpent when the sun catches its waters. As the path veers to the south west towards Holme House Fell, some of Bowland's finest scenery unfolds. The hillscape is remote, quiet and seemingly free from man's influences-not even a fence to mar the view. A retrospective gaze across the tight interlocking spurs of Fiendsdale and the folds of more distant Bowland Fells reveals the distinctive outlines of Ingleborough on the horizon.

Eventually the impressive waters of Fiendsdale become but a trickle on gravelly beds amongst the peat haggs of the watershed. The path becomes less distinct, although cairns make it discernible even in hill fog. A fence on the ridge, which leads the way to Fair Snape's highest point, is crossed twice but, in mist, it is advisable to follow its line more closely. The ensuing mile is marshy and covered with peat haggs making progress more laboured than one would expect for a ridge but it is an airy region with views of the Lancashire coast and with the objective, Fair Snape maintaining the interest in views ahead.

There is an intersection of fences at the 1707 foot summit. If the fence leading off to the right is followed to the point when it changes direction to the south east, a compass bearing of 250° will lead to the second and more popular summit.

There are new views from this second summit. We are in the midst of a circle of fells which enclose the Bleasdale

Fiendsdale

Estate, where a complex network of fields, farms, country lanes and small woods are divided by the winding sylvan dene of the River Brock. The harsher outlines of a dark conifer plantation distort the contours of Oakenclough Fell to the west. Parlick, which is seen from this angle as a shapely minion, leads the eye to southern vistas which include Beacon Fell, swelling from the surrounding farmlands and capped with the dark spread of sitka spruce. Beyond it ,vast plains, interrupted by the Ribble Estuary and town of Preston, fade into a pale blue haze on the horizon.

ROUTE 7
FAIR SNAPE from Saddle End, Chipping

Distance 3 miles (one way) - moderate

Of the southern approaches to Fair Snape, this is by far the best as it misses the eroded slopes of Parlick and gives pleasant views of the Hodder Valley.

A concrete lane leads from ref. 616448 to Saddle End Farm where a firm track continues in the same direction before turning northwards on the slopes of Saddle Fell. After passing through a gate onto the open fellsides, the access area is entered and, on most days, we are free to roam. The track becomes less obvious as it levels out to the west of Burnslack but is re-established on the next rise when it becomes a groove in pale grassy slopes. Retrospective views improve as height is gained. Always prominent beyond the attractive bowl of the Burnslack Valley are the twin escarpments of Longridge Fell

Descending Saddle Fell

and the more distant Pendle Hill. The latter can be distinguished beyond the smoky plume of the West Bradford

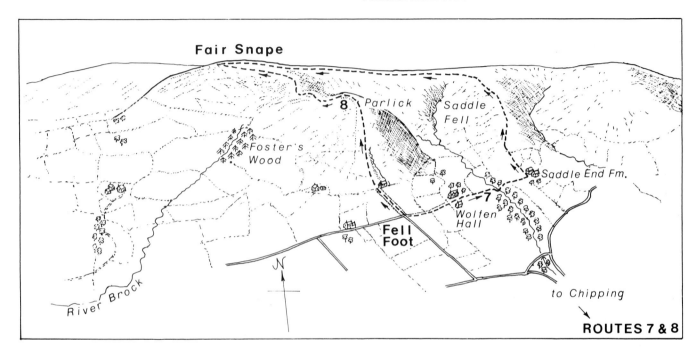

Fair Snape

8

Parlick

Saddle Fell

Foster's Wood

Saddle End Fm.

7

Wolfen Hall

Fell Foot

N

River Brock

to Chipping

ROUTES 7 & 8

Cement Works near Clitheroe. To the west Parlick is centre-stage, towering above the seemingly diminutive buildings of Wolfen Hall and rising in rough slopes from a wild hollow un-named by the map-makers.

As the track approaches the ridge it veers westwards at the head of this hollow offering an easy route through rough peat-hagged terrain (the ridge to Totridge Fell in the east is one of the roughest in Bowland). The 'green road', which has carried us thus far, terminates at the ridge fence just short of Fair Snape's north eastern summit (1707), where there is an intersection of fences. To reach the more popular western summit, follow the fence leading south eastwards until it changes direction (SSE) thence assume a bearing of 250° as in the Langden Castle route.

ROUTE 8
FAIR SNAPE FELL AND PARLICK FROM FELL FOOT

Distance- 2³/₄ miles (one way) a stiff but short climb

This is the most popular route to Fair Snape Fell and it shows. Parlick's proud Pike looms large above the newly renovated cottage of Fell Foot, but its slopes have been eroded by the masses who have scaled the fells for walking, hang-gliding or fell-running. I was not going to include a route in the book but it is the obvious route for those who just want to climb to Parlick and the succeeding ridge to Fair Snape is a joy to walk.

There are tracks which meekly skirt the fell but the best coarse is a bold one straight ahead to the skyline with the eroded chasm of an un-named clough to the right. Although it is less than a third of a mile between Fell Foot and Parlick's summit, few will do it without a brief rest to relieve the protesting lungs and calf muscles. On reaching the top, all the efforts are supremely rewarded with extensive and contrasting panoramas. To the north, the palid mountain grasses cling to the sleek weather-beaten slopes of Wolf Fell and Fair Snape, which rises from an undulating ridge. In the opposite direction, the intricate designs formed by winding country lanes, hedgerows ,scattered farmhouses and copses compose a gentle more verdant landscape. This is the Vale of Chipping and epitomizes our "green and pleasant land".

Beyond Parlick, the stride can be lengthened for the route which has now been transformed into a delightful ridge walk. The track is laid before you descending at first to the hollow of Nick's Chair, before climbing to the left on Fair Snape, whose smoothly contoured slopes are etched by a zig-zag path climbing from Bleasdale. (not a right of way unfortunately!)

A fence guides early progress from Parlick but, at ref. 597464, a cairned path leads NNW on firm ground to the hills superior western summit. For those preferring to go directly to the higher eastern summit, just follow the fence to the highest ground marked by an intersection of fences and pile of stones.

N.B. This route could be combined with the Saddle End route to form a circular.

ROUTE 9
FAIR SNAPE FELL from Bleasdale Post Office

Distance 5 miles (one way) moderate to hard

Bleasdale Post Office lies four miles to the west of Chipping on a minor leafy lane in a pleasant corner sandwiched between Beacon Fell and the higher moors rising to Fair Snape. It is also a cafe offering a good selection of cakes, beverages and hot meals - quite a boon after a hard day's walk on the fells! This route to Fair Snape Fell is one of the more popular and meets the one already described from the Trough at Holme House Fell on the watershed above Fiendsdale.

Fair Snape from Parlick

On the Hornby Road approaching the old county border fence

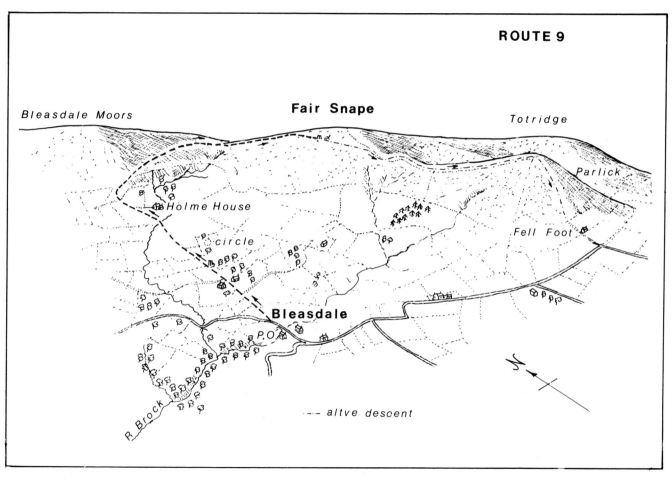

ROUTE 9

Bleasdale Moors

Fair Snape

Totridge

Parlick

Holme House

Fell Foot

circle

Bleasdale

P.O.

R. Brock

N

--- altve descent

Parlick from Fair Snape

A narrow metalled lane leads northwards from ref. 573447 close to the Post Office and leads to the quiet hamlet of Bleasdale, passing first the little school on the left and then St. Eadmer's Church, which was built in 1835 on the site of a medieval church.

A track then continues northwards passing through rich farmlands. To the right are the grassy flanks of Fair Snape and Parlick, whilst ahead are those of the Bleasdale fells which will gain us our entry to the ridge.

The Bleasdale area is known to have been inhabited in the bronze age and, at ref. 577460, set amongst a small copse, is the Bleasdale Circle which dates back to about 1800BC. Concrete pillars mark the position of the original wooden posts, the remains of which can be seen in the Harris Museum at Preston along with two urns from the same period. Unfortunately there is no right of way to enable the general public to visit the site which is in the grounds of Vicarage Farm (ref. 574459).

There is a fork in the tracks at ref. 576463. One goes to Holme House Farm and is not a right of way although many people seem to use it as such. The correct left fork leads to Admarsh Barn Farm, where a path leads NNW across fields, crossing a footbridge en route back to the original farm track to the north west of Holme House Farm. A few yards further on the track turns sharp left and the path is taken directly ahead for the Bleasdale fellsides.

A gate in the dry stone wall to the north leads the way eastwards to the open fellsides of the access area. You are free to roam. From here a well defined path rakes up the hillside giving ever widening southern views over the Lancashire Plains. Fair Snape appears from this vantage to be a steep sided grassy escarpment soaring from the pastures of Bleasdale. When the watershed is reached on the top Holme House Fell, new views appear of Bowland's northern fells including Ward's Stone, White Hill and Whins Brow. Over their tops, if the atmosphere is clear, Ingleborough and Pen-y-Ghent will be discernible.

The way to Fair Snape's summit is southwards across a glutinous peaty ridge and is described in detail in the Trough Route (No. 7)

St. Eadmer's Bleasdale

THE LONELY VALLEYS

O.S. Landranger maps 1:50000 Nos 102 & 103

Route 10 The Hornby Road- High Salter to Croasdale
Route 11 Whitendale and Brennand

Bowland has many lovely wide pastoral valleys drained by meandering rivers with superb footpaths for Sunday strolls but the ones included in this section are far removed. They are the wild remote valleys, cut by young ,fast flowing streams that have escaped from the clutches of the glutinous peat of their moorland sources. They are the valleys which lead into the quiet seclusion of Bowland's heartlands. This is a fellwalkers' book and these are fell walks of the highest order. Good views are afforded of the high peaks that are otherwise 'out of bounds' - Wolf Stones, White Hill and Middle Knoll - the list is endless. At the very least you can get an idea of what you are missing!

ROUTE 10
THE HORNBY ROAD   Croasdale to High Salter

Distance 9 miles (one way) - moderate

Described by the much loved A.W. Wainwright as "possibly the finest moorland walk in England", this is definitely one of the best in the book. It reaches no mountain summits but visits beautiful remote moors and little known vales, miles from modern civilisation .

Although it is possible to undertake a return journey, this walk is best made by a small group leaving cars at either end of the journey.

The old Hornby Road begins from Slaidburn but it is better to take the car to ref.693549 beneath Low Fell. The spot, which is generally regarded as the termination of the road, proper, is easily recognised. A five-barred gate spans the road which bends sharp right to circumvent the high moorland beyond. There is room at the roadside for a couple of cars either side of the gate.

The old road beyond the gate has been metalled, but the tarmac is now crumbling and is unlikely to be replaced. In views to the south, Pendle Hill dominates rising from the Ribble Valley behind the lower and greener Waddington Fell, distinguished by a radio mast.

The road veers to the left into the wild valley of Croasdale and passes the New Bridge (ref.686561), which spans Black Brook, a tributary of Croasdale Brook, some two hundred feet below. A good pace can be made on the firm stony track which passes quarry workings on the shoulder of Baxton Fell. The numbered stone shelter-like constructions are shooters' hides. Prominent in the landscape from here are the southern flanks of White Hill, which are riven by deep cloughs and adorned with the scattered crags, known as the

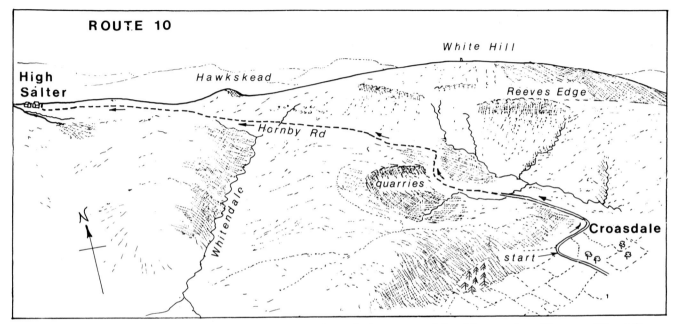

Bull Stones, and fringed by the craggy Reeves Edge. As the wide stony track climbs through heathery slopes, an old building on the horizon becomes increasingly distinct. It is, in fact, an old shooters' hut perched high on the hillside just above the old road and with wide views of all the hunting grounds.

As the head of Croasdale is passed, another high and lonely valley appears to the left. This is Whitendale. The wandering Whitendale River can be seen threading between the interwoven fells of Baxton, the oddly named Good Greave and the rounded Middle Knoll.

A strangely shaped summit catches the eye to the west. It appears as a diminutive diadem, a rocky crest perched conspicuously on its vast moorland shoulders. This is Wolfhole Crag, a romantically named fell, a Siren tempting the walker to stray from the track. Alas, it is out of bounds!

The fence marking the watershed at the head of Whitendale is that of the old county boundary between Lancashire and

The Hornby Road and Roeburndale

Yorkshire but, since 1974, we are well and truly in the Red Rose domain. This section of the track is predictably the boggiest but it is easily negotiated .

A third valley, Roeburndale is encountered beyond the county fence. It is flanked by Mallowdale Fell,whose slopes are cut by a dozen or so streams running parallel. Sometimes they are dry but after rainfall they are impressively seen as white, foaming torrents scurrying down the dark fells to join the mother Roeburn. A remote stony shooters' track can also be seen climbing high on the slopes of Mallowdale.

Hawkshead is the outlying fell to the north of the Hornby Road and, once it has been passed, wide views across Ribblesdale to the Three Peaks and Craven Hills are revealed for the first time. Also seen in the same wide sweep are Morecambe Bay and the Lakeland Hills. Trees are seen on the valley floor and the scene is transformed from ochre to emerald; wild to cultivated. Then we are confronted with a large farm and scattered trees. This is High Salter Farm at journeys end!

ROUTE 11
WHITENDALE AND BRENNAND via Dunsop Fell and Whins Brow

Distance 6^1/$_2$ mile (14 with return route via Dunsop Bridge)- moderate (one way) -hard (circular)

In the wild valleys of Whitendale and Brennand at the heart of Bowland's high fell country, generations of farmers have created, from their toils, emerald and fertile pastures. These are like oasis' in a desert of high inhospitable hillscapes.

The walk I have devised to cross these beautiful valleys starts at map reference 693549 by the old Hornby Road and finishes on the Trough Road at 627524. It is best to have a car at either end, but it is possible to make it into a circular walk by using the road south eastwards to Dunsop Fell and thence across pastoral land by the flanks of Burn Fell. Cars can be left in a few places by the narrow tarmac lane north of Higher Wood House but care must be exercised in order not to hamper farming activities.

A rutted track climbs westwards up the slopes of Dunsop Fell giving, retrospective views of the Stocks Reservoir, which is surrounded by spruce woods. The high escarpment of Pendle Hill looms large on the southern horizon, although its lower slopes are obscured by Waddington Fell, which can easily be recognised by the presence of its tall radio mast. Often plumes of white smoke can be seen between the two fells originating from the cement works of West Bradford (invisible from hereabouts). The broad, flat top of Dunsop Fell, known as Dunsop Head, is grassy although an area to the north is covered by the usual Bowland peat haggs. The path, now sketchy and a little marshy in places, is marked by well spaced posts which reassure the walker that he is on the right track and the landowners that their grouse moors are only minimally being encroached upon. The apparent close proximity of the other high Bowland Hills was surprising to me

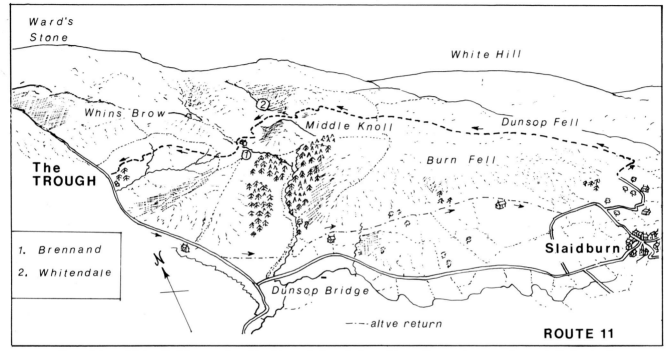

Ward's Stone

White Hill

Whins Brow

Middle Knoll

Dunsop Fell

The TROUGH

Burn Fell

1. Brennand
2. Whitendale

N

Slaidburn

Dunsop Bridge

- - altve return

ROUTE 11

opon my first visit and I dwelled longer than I had intended, picking out routes of previous escapades. First to catch the eye was the noble form of Totridge with Fair Snape's sweeping whaleback ridge behind. Further north in an arc of fells were Ward's Stone and Wolfhole Crag. As the path descended beyond the dry-stone summit wall, two more shapely fells appeared. The nearer one was lower, but its proud steep slopes, indented by a diagonal strata of crag.defied onlookers to say that it was inferior. This was Middle Knoll and, from all directions, it tempts walkers to stray from their chosen routes. Lying behind and partially obscured is its taller neighbour, Whins Brow which, from this angle, is broad, sparsely cragged and rent by a deep clough.

As it nears Whitendale, the path becomes a ribbon-like

swathe through a carpet of heather and is punctuated by stone cairns and tall waymarking posts. When the farm of Whitendale does appear beyond the concave Dunsop slopes it is seen in a splendid setting - a revelation! When one sees the wildness of the surroundings, it is difficult to imagine that they can be tamed yet here there are green velvet pastures beneath the barren hillslopes and a pleasant farmhouse shaded by two small enclosures of mixed woodland. Higher up the valley amongst rougher pastures are a couple of new spruce plantations which will not spoil the appeal of the scene as long as they are not expanded.

Just preceding the farm, the path meets a stony cart-track which zig-zags past modern store buildings and through the farmyard to reach a modern metalled lane. A small footbridge, immediately opposite, is crossed before an assault is made on extremely steep grassy slopes, which rise to the col between Middle Knoll and Lee End. Higher Laithe (Laithe means barn), a ruined building commands attention, in views to the north. It is situated in high, lush green fields, and dwarfed by the precipitous flanks of Whitendale Fell.

The terrain at the col is quite marshy and the path threads through an area of dense reeds. The Brennand Valley gives up its secret beauty slowly on the descent. All is revealed beyond a primitive stile over a dry-stone wall. The stony track which follows focuses the attention on Brennand Farm, the centre-stage of a beautiful verdant arena set below the wild, barren terraces of Whins Brow. The green pastures rise gingerly on its flanks and attention is drawn to yet another Higher

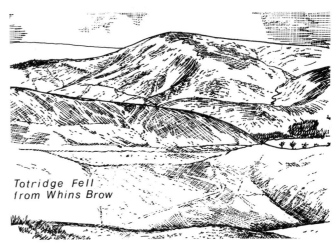

Totridge Fell from Whins Brow

Laithe, this time in full repair.

Before reaching the farm, the stony track leads down to and crosses the Brennand River. A right turn at the farmhouse is followed by a south-westerly course across fields. The waymarked path heads towards the crags between Whins Brow and Whin Fell. On the rougher slopes beyond the farm's cultivated pastures, a faint track, known as Ouster Rake, is used to make SSE for the ridge. At this point we are less than half a mile from the summit, which is well worth a detour (a harmless trespass except on shooting days). The view northwards from the summit across Swine Clough is superb - Bowland's finest single vista! The gash of the clough leads the eye to the pattern of green fields that rise from the dwarfed farm buildings of Brennand to the col between the rough fells of Lee End and Middle Knoll. Middle Knoll looks as appealing as ever with its steep green slopes and flat peaty cap. Waves of fells lie beyond. Firstly the tops of Whitendale and Baxton Fells then the long ridge between Ward's Stone and White Hill. If the atmosphere is clear then Whernside, Ingleborough and Pen-y-Ghent will peer on the horizon over the tops of these Bowland hills.

After retracing steps to the right of way, a distinct path leads SSW to ford Rams Clough before crossing westwards beneath the 'brow'. A small copse by the ruins of Trough House is passed and from here a rutted track leads to the Trough Road two and a half miles west of Dunsop Bridge.

ROUTE BACK TO THE STARTING POINT

The undulating Trough Road is not an unpleasant way to walk, although it is a bit busy in high summer. It is followed south-eastwards to ref. 651506, where a path traversing fields leads to the Dunsop Valley road. A brief northbound course is made to 657509. Here a footbridge is used to cross the lively river, whose surrounding hillslopes have been distorted and submerged in a sea of spruce. The route ascends north east to Beatrix Farm and then across farmlands lying beneath the long escarpment of Burn Fell until Burn House, where a path leads south-eastwards to reach a country lane at ref. 688525. This can be followed to Higher Wood House, 1 miles distant.

Brennand Valley

PENDLE HILL
by Phil Iddon

O.S. Landranger Map 1:50000 No. 103

Route 12 From Pendleside
Route 13 From Ogden Clough
Route 14 From The Nick of Pendle
Route 15 From Worston

Pendle Hill rises proud from rural pastures south of the Ribble Valley and to the north of the industrial plains surrounding the sprawling urban conurbations of Burnley, Nelson and Colne. It has a unique magnetism not least derived from its position and shape. Standing alone, the imposing and noble form of this whaleback escarpment predominates the land for miles around. In the days before modern instruments were absent and a large degree of guesswork had to be relied upon, Pendle Hill was thought to be one of England's highest hills at over three thousand four hundred feet! This gross overestimation highlights its truer impression on the landscape, which belies its actual height of eighteen-hundred and thirty-one feet.

The villages of Newchurch, Sabden, Barley and Downham all nestle around the base of the hill and, from each of these places, Pendle assumes different and distinctive profiles. Its full grandeur and transcendence over its environment can be appreciated best from Downham where its great flank, seemingly always in shadow, looms menacingly over the village, giving the impression of a razor sharp ridge. Early in the morning, before cars or other contemporary contraptions wake from their sleep, and when smoke rises gently from the chimneys of the stone cottages, the whole scene assumes a timeless aura, as though plucked from another century.

Pendle Hill comprises the moors of Pendle, Barley Mearley Spence and Pendleton and together they cover an expanse of twenty square miles. To the north and east are escarpments which contrast with its generally undulating nature. Several cloughs interrupt the moors, two of which, Mearley and Ogden, provide access to the summit. Ogden, the largest and most rugged, and shaped like the blade of a sickle, almost cuts the hill in two. It provides the water catchment for the two reservoirs situated in its lower regions near the village of Barley.

The majority of Pendle's surface is peat - boggy and wet in parts, but seldom a problem for the walker. The peat is covered mainly by rough grass and, to a lesser extent, heather and bilberry. Its core is of millstone grit with underlying strata of limestone which surface at Worsaw Hill near Downham. On the northern slopes and the summit, the gritstone has been exposed and provides firmer conditions underfoot.

The summit lies at the north eastern end of the hill. Historically it was part of a system of beacons, where a great

Dawn at Downham looking towards Pendle's 'big end'

fire would be lit to summon the yeoman of the district to arms, to fight for their peers. In less turbulent times a lookout would be posted to watch for bad weather so that a warning could be given to haymakers in the fields below of approaching storms or rain clouds. Now the summit is most valued by the walker who is afforded a wonderful 360° panorama comprising agricultural plains, industrial townscapes, the Irish Sea coastline and the distant hills of Yorkshire and the Lake District.

Pendle is at its most dramatic in the winter months when, stripped of its colourful vegetation, it is rendered bare with dark, monochrome shades accentuating its eerie mood. A peculiar characteristic, the Snow Witch, occurs when the winter snows recede leaving only the deepest snow lying in the northern gullies. The unmistakable image of a witch is formed. The tall, pointed hat and long flowing robes leave little to the imagination ,providing an uncanny reminder of the hill's historical associations with witchcraft.

ROUTE 12
PENDLE HILL from Pendleside

Distance 1$\frac{1}{4}$ miles (one way) - fairly easy

The direct ascent of Pendle's Big End from Pendleside is the shortest route to the summit and is thus an ideal walk for a summer's evening or when time is short during the winter months. It begins at ref. 815416 from the high lane that connects the villages of Barley and Downham. A track is followed south westwards toward the hill's eastern facade, passing the farm of Pendleside. Just before a second dwelling, Pendle House, which lies at the end of the lane and at the very foot of the escarpment, the track is abandoned and the route continues north westwards alongside a dry-stone wall.

The farmlands are left behind beyond a kissing gate, where a well used track rises on the threshold of the high hillside. In winter this section is prone to severe icing and care must be exercised on the ascent. Within a short distance the path divides offering three routes. The one to the left skirts the base of the escarpment towards the Ogden Reservoirs whilst the middle one forges a direct and steep passage to the summit. The third and most well defined track is to the right and offers the best approach revealing more varied aspects of the hill.Unfortunately,in the lower regions,the path has been in the

hands of the 'improvers' who,in order to halt the scars of erosion have constructed an unnatural paved surface inflicting, in the process, their own scars. Another cruel blow to the hill's dignity is the addition of pathside bench seats which surely have no place in a wilderness environment.

The path climbs steeply through bilberries and also dense ferns which in autumn sunlight add a flame coloured cloak to the landscape. The steepness of the path relents as the rocky gritstone outcrop at the edge of the summit plateau is reached. We are now on Pendle's famous Big End and look across a vast area of moorland plateau. The route to the summit is but a stroll southwards across these high ,airy moors.

Pendle Hill's isolated position means that it offers its

Scout Cairn, Pendle Hill

climbers wonderful unbroken panoramas of surrounding countryside and more distant fells. In views northwards across the Ribble plains are the Craven Hills of Yorkshire which rise to the unmistakable profiles of Ingleborough, Whernside and Pen-y-Ghent. To the south are the industrial towns of Nelson, Burnley and Colne with the power station cooling towers of Padiham dominating the myriad rooftops at their feet. Beyond the towns are the rounded moors of the South Pennines. The chequered field patterns in the pastoral prospect to the east are broken by the two small Black Moss Reservoirs and distorted by the contours of the rolling lower hills. The curiosity is aroused when Blacko Tower, perched on one of these lower fells, is sighted. The fifty foot tower was built in 1890 for Jonathan Stansfield, a wealthy grocer, who mistakenly be-

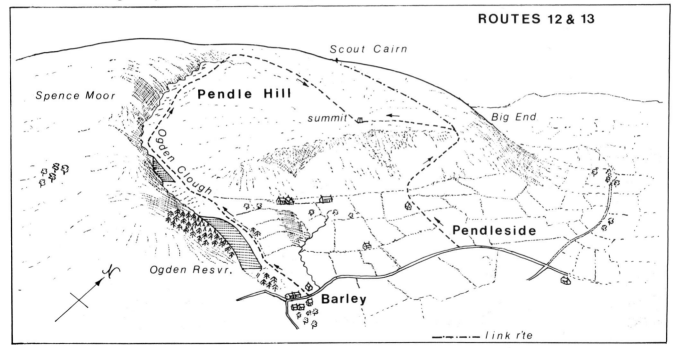

ROUTES 12 & 13

Scout Cairn

Spence Moor

Pendle Hill

summit

Big End

Ogden Clough

Pendleside

Ogden Resvr.

Barley

— · — · — link r'te

lieved it would fulfil his desire to see all of Ribblesdale. Alas, in practice, he was wrong! Perhaps he should have walked to the summit of Pendle.

Route 13
PENDLE HILL FROM BARLEY Via Ogden Clough

Distance 4^1/$_2$ miles (one way) - moderate to hard

This is the most rewarding route that Pendle has to offer for Ogden is the wildest and most rugged of its cloughs and reaches deep into the hill, its source being very close to the summit itself.

The public car park on the outskirts of Barley village provides a convenient starting place and ,at ref.823403, a metalled cul-de-sac from the main road leads to a cart track, which in turn climbs west to Barley Green. It then passes the larger of Ogden's two reservoirs which were built to supply Nelson with its drinking water. By its southern shores are the dark conifers of Fell Wood which partially cloak the pastures of Sadlers Heights (not marked on 1:50000 maps). To the north of the path, Pendle Hill's steep eastern facade rises boldly above the scattered high fell farms that shelter at its feet.

The path continues past the Upper Ogden Reservoir above the northern banks of the Ogden Clough. The Spence and Barley Moors soon converge, casting their shadows over the stream to form a wild, ravine, which shuts out views and sounds from the world outside Pendle. Wild life abounds hereabouts - if you're lucky, you may see a fox slinking

silently across the shaded slopes. As the clough gradually arcs northwards, Pendle's most quiet inner reaches are entered. The silence of this desolate lonely moorland is only disturbed by the sound of the playful stream, the song of a skylark or shrill cry of a grouse.

The clough becomes shallow, petering out on the open

Above Ogden Clough, Pendle Hill

Brennand Valley from Whins Brow

Pendle Hill from the north

moorland to the west of the summit. The stream becomes more sedate and is crossed near to its source at a place marked by pile of stones on its opposite banks. The peat ruts which cover the ground ahead can, after wet weather, deteriorate into a quagmire and the peace of the moor may be disturbed by the ribald oratory of walkers impatiently trying to extricate themselves from knee deep black sludge. The perils of this terrain, however, can be avoided by intelligent circumventions and, on reaching terra firma once more, a clearly defined track will lead to the fair summit of this grand old hill.

Route 14
PENDLE HILL from the Nick of Pendle

Distance 3^1/2 miles (one way) - easy

The Nick of Pendle lies on the high pass between Pendle Hill and Wiswell Moor and is traversed by the narrow lane which connects Clitheroe with the village of Sabden. The route, which commences here is one of the longer ones to Pendle's summit, but the starting point, like Pendleside, is high above sea level. The ascent is also very gradual and thus it requires little physical exertion. It is best saved for calm conditions however, as the path adheres close to the escarpment's edge and is exposed to the elements.

A broad track leaves the road near to the car park (ref.773386) and leads north east across the bronze age burial site of Apronfull Hill. This, according to local legend, is where the Devil collected an apronfull of stones and bombarded Clitheroe Castle, breaching the wall of its keep and creating an opening named the Devil's Window. To the left of the path, the land steeply falls away to the deep and yawning Ashdean Clough, which leads the eye westwards beyond the shapely knoll of Wiswell Moor to the plains of the Ribble Valley and estuary.

The gradient becomes steeper on reaching the plateau to the north west of Spence Moor, whose expanses are rent by the serpentine Ogden Clough. The edge of the broad moorlands is followed past the head of Ashdean Clough onto Pendle Moor, which is divided by Mearley Clough. Here the path joins the Worston route.

ROUTE 15
PENDLE HILL from Worston

Distance 4 miles (one way) - moderate

The small village of Worston, just off the busy A59 on Pendle's northern side, is a good place to start an ascent which visits Mearley Clough, a quiet, undiscovered corner of the fell.

From the village, a tree-lined winding lane is leads to ref.780427 where the approach lane to Moorside is followed until it turns eastwards. Here a path, which links the many farms at Pendle's foot, is traced southwards past the farm buildings of Angram Green. The steep slopes of the hill are highlighted by deep swathing gullies, no doubt a product

Mearley Clough, Pendle Hill looking across Clitheroe to the hills of Bowland

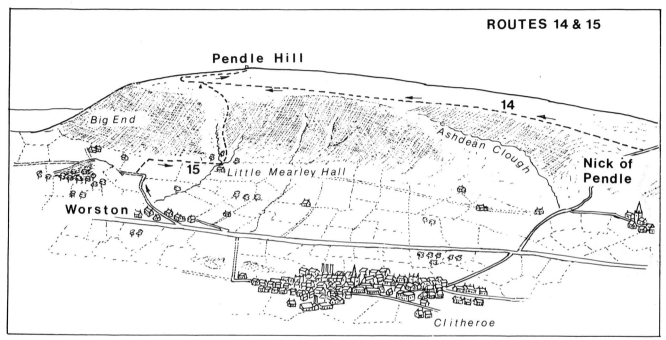

of flooding, which from time to time troubles the land hereabouts. On raising the eyes to the outline of the moor, Scout Cairn will be seen at the highest point, towering loftily a thousand feet above.

After reaching the sixteenth century Little Mearley Hall, a left turn is made on a wide track through the mature woodland at the foot of Mearley Clough. Beyond the woods, the track narrows and soon it enters a wild and surprisingly dramatic scene of the hidden clough - deep and dark. It is an outstanding facet of Pendle's character, worthy of appreciation before continuing along the steep slopes to the right of the stream. The ground here is covered with loose gritstone and for most of the time shielded from sunlight.

At the head of the clough, the sparse vegetation is replaced by the course grasses, which clothe most of the hills upper reaches. The path rises north eastwards along the escarpment's edge until Scout Cairn is reached. The cairn, nine feet high and five feet in diameter, was built to commemorate seventy years of scouting and has views at least equal to the summit itself. Distant views of the Craven Hills are similar but those of the Ribble Valley are improved. The town and castle of Clitheroe, bask in rich and fertile farmland surroundings, leading the eye past the gentle and verdant escarpment of Longridge Fell towards the wild Bowland Hills. On a clear day, beyond the Fylde Coast (complete with Blackpool Tower) and the inlet of Morecambe Bay, are the pale but still recognisable angular peaks of Lakeland.

Half a mile to the east of Scout Cairn, the path passes a large stone shelter before reaching the north-eastern extremities of the plateau. Here a dry-stone wall, known as Robin Hood's Wall, is straddled via a large ladder stile and the southerly course used on the ascent from Pendleside is taken to the summit.

SOUTH PENNINES

The South Pennines are an area of wild and craggy moors between the Yorkshire Dales and the Peak District. The rock from which they are formed, like Bowland, is millstone grit. This consists of sandstones and shales and is naturally gold,but oxidises to form an inky black surface. (aided and catalysed by the soot and grime exuded by factory chimneys in Victorian times.) Glyn Hughes in his brilliant book of Pennine travels, *Millstone Grit*, likened the rock to the local people by writing :-

"The millstone grit defines also the nature of the people who dwell on it. Rough, truculent and dour they may appear, but this , as with their stone is only a forbidding exterior ; break it open, and, just as the millstone grit is gold inside, so these people sparkle with humour courage and kindness".

The highest fell in the South Pennines at 1696 ft.is Boulsworth Hill, known to some as Lad Law, the name of its summit. As would be expected,the views from this summit are unrivalled within the group. From most of the tops you will find yourself picking out distant towns as well as neighbouring hills for this is the nature of the area. Its neighbour, Black Hameldon, is probably the marshiest of the group although this should not put you off for the walks to it are some of the best and wildest in the book. The steep sided deans around Hebden Bridge are filled with oak, birch and pine and make an excellent preamble for the spartan higher moors. The circular route I have included to High Brown Knoll descends via

Lund Tower, Wolf Stones

Crimsworth Dean and is a marvellous example of the superb contrasts between valley and tops.

Part of the attraction of the South Pennines results from their industrial heritage. Until the industrial revolution, the

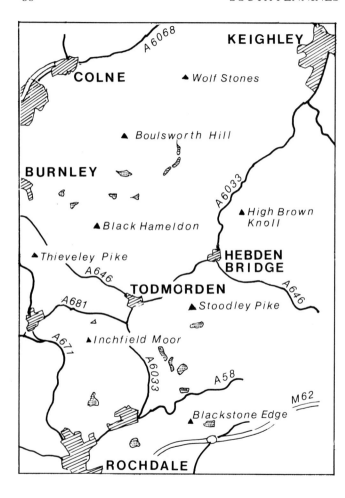

valleys, which are now the domain of modern industry, were very marshy and thickly afforested. The villages, farms, mills and cottages were all higher on the hillsides, as were the interlinking roads or 'causeways', usually paved with slabs of millstone grit. The communities such as Mankinholes, Heptonstall and Wycoller are thus far older than Todmorden, Burnley and Colne, whose fortunes were propagated by the coming of the railways and canals. Although the older communities have dwindled in size and many of their mills and mines have decayed or ceased production, the often obscure relics remain.

The largest landowners must be the Water Authorities and this gives cause for concern for many of the concessionary paths agreed with the old Water Board could be withdrawn or become 'toll Paths'. It is to be hoped that the new companies, which have been substantially financed by French corporations, do not asset strip our heritage by selling off the land for development, for one has to say that it makes financial sense!

Many fell-walkers have been introduced to the area by the Pennine Way, which visits Blackstone Edge, Stoodley Pike, Withins Height and Wolf Stones (rarely along the most rewarding routes). Some of these walkers return but many are too magnetised by the more majestic peaks further north. Its a shame, for they will have missed the magnificent views from Boulsworth Hill the weird crags of Brides Stones, the beautiful deans around Hebden Bridge and the remoteness of Black Hameldon. These more subtle charms belong to the South Pennines.

BLACKSTONE EDGE

O.S. Landranger Map (1:50000) No. 109 or
Outdoor Leisure Map (1:25000) No.21 'South Pennines'

Route 16 Circular from Hollingworth Lake
Route 17 From the Windy Hill Radio Mast

Blackstone Edge, which was once described by Daniel Defoe, creator of Robinson Crusoe, as "the Andes of the north', is situated between the vast conurbations of Greater Manchester and Huddersfield. Here the Pennine Chain is at its narrowest and is parcelled by the arterial highways of the M62, A58 and A672 which climb high passes over bare moors separating cities to the east and west.

In fact another highway, an ancient, well preserved Roman road , crosses Blackstone Edge between Lydgate and Rishworth Moor to the north of the summit. This one , however offers more tranquillity away from the motor car and makes a superb pathway to the main ridge.

Blackstone Edge belongs to Littleborough in the same way as Stoodley Pike does to Todmorden. It stands guardian to the inhabitants sheltering them from cruel eastern winds and its high crags can be seen from the town's pavements. The lower western slopes are cultivated, enclosed by stone walls and divided by a series of twisting sylvan glens. On these lower slopes lies Hollingworth Lake, an old reservoir, now given up to the interests of recreation.

On the boundary between the cultivated lands and open moors, a line of electricity pylons mars the attractiveness of the scene but, above the pale grassy knolls of Clegg Moor and on the horizon, the craggy millstone grit outcrops proudly

The Aiggin Stone

The Roman Road, Blackstone Edge with Hollingworth Lake and Littleborough in the distance

crown the hillsides to form Blackstone Edge. The summit is a glorious place - the giant crags and boulders, which border an area of firm, reddish peat, offer an excellent platform to view airy western panoramas.

Blackstone Edge's eastern flanks are of less importance to the walker, being largely featureless. The marshy slopes are drained by the Green Withens Reservoir,a lonely desolate high lake. Far more harsh are the glutinous peat swamps of Redmires, which still form a barrier to easy passage along the Pennine Way even though the track across them has been improved in recent years.

In conclusion, if I were asked to pinpoint Blackstone Edge's finest attribute, I would have to say that it was its panoramic western view, which encompasses intricate patterns of high hill and urban valley surrounding the vast plains which pale to the Manchester horizon.

ROUTE 16
BLACKSTONE EDGE - A Circular from Hollingworth Lake

Distance 7 miles- moderate

Hollingworth Lake was built around 1800 to maintain water levels in the Rochdale Canal. Nowadays it is at the heart of an immensely popular Country Park and Nature Reserve. From its shores, the serrated gritstone crest of Blackstone Edge can be seen on the horizon beyond the rolling flanks of Clegg Moor. There are two routes from here to the summit and both can be combined in a circular walk ,which is at its best on a late Spring afternoon when the cottage gardens and woodlands of the Lakeside area are ablaze with the colour of a myriad blooms and the descending sun shines obliquely across the crags to highlight the hill's noble form.

From the car park (ref. 939153), a track leads north-eastwards past trees,which line the foot of Cleggswood Hill. When it turns right ,it is abandoned for a flagged path which continues north-eastwards, traversing a field where picnic benches border a quiet stream. A narrow footbridge,with gates at both ends,then leads across the stream, whose banks are followed through attractive and verdant countryside. Small rounded hills, parcelled by dry-stone walls, are fringed with deciduous woodland, resplendent with wild flowers. Lane Foot Farm (ref. 945160 - not named on 1;50000 maps) is pleasantly situated at the head of two sylvan vales, and by it, the path converges with one from the Littleborough suburb of Ealees. Our route then continues by the stream, which it crosses,before passing to the north of the impressively named cottage of Owlet Hall . From here a farm road skirts the local golf course to Shaw Lane Farm (ref. 953160) beyond which a wide stony track (bridleway) is encountered. This roughly traces the north-south line of electricity pylons on the edge of the open fellsides and is followed northwards to Lydgate, where a few cottages are huddled together by a minor road threading between two rounded, grassy hills.

To the north of the cottages, the Blackstone Edge Roman Road begins as an inconspicuous worn path climbing

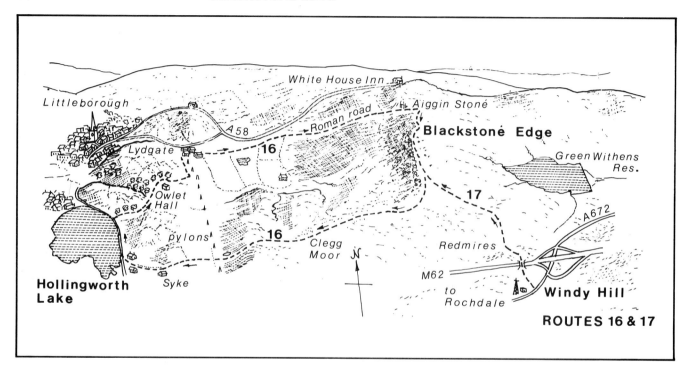

ROUTES 16 & 17

eastwards over the grassy lower hillslopes. It is bordered by a dry-stone wall which guides it to a point close to the A58 road. The busy highway meanders to the horizon over the high moors ahead. In retrospective views, Hollingworth lake can be seen in its entirety surrounded by grassy knolls, cultivated pastures and dotted farmhouses. Further north, rising beyond the dwellings of Littleborough, are the barren slopes of Shore Moor. The view ahead is not without its appeal either. Velvet fields rise in gentle curves to the high farm of Blackstone Edge Fold lying in a lonely combe beneath the rough moorland that soars to the rocky crest of Blackstone Edge.

As the road gains height, it becomes more defined and,

on approaching a water board leat, paving slabs of millstone grit appear with increasing regularity until it is seen in all its well-preserved glory. Now sixteen foot wide it's flags are complete and divided at the centre with a prominent drainage channel.

The ancient road attains the ridge by an old guide post known as the Aiggin Stone, whose main slab has remained collapsed for years. To the west, occupying a hollow beneath dull declining moors, is the Green Withens Reservoir, which looks at its best in the hazy morning sun, when it appears as a shimmering luminous sheet amongst palid ethereal hillslopes.

A cairned path climbs southwards across a terrain of firm peat and heather towards the summit which is crowned with many curiously shaped crags and outcrops overlooking its bouldery western flanks. The crags make excellent perches on which to admire the superb panoramas which have unfolded. The pale and empty moorland declines to farm pastures at the edge of the vast plains of Greater Manchester which are punctuated by tower blocks and chimneys as far as the eye can see. To the north west of the plain lies Littleborough, its proud church spire towering above a sea of stone terraces crowded by Shore Moor, whose empty slopes contrast with the alien red-tiled houses of a recent housing estate. To the north of the summit, across a flat plateau on which four reservoirs have been built, the monument on Stoodley Pike can be seen preceding more distant views over Heptonstall Moor to Boulsworth Hill.

For the descent, the line of crags is followed southwards, ignoring the cairned Pennine Way path, which veers to the left (SE) towards Redmires. Prominent in views ahead are the G.P.O.'s Windy Hill Mast and the bustling M62 Trans-Pennine motorway. From the most southerly crags a trackless south-western course is taken across rough grassy terrain which is surprisingly firm, except after really wet weather. At ref. 970155, a narrow path commences and traces the northern edge of Clegg Moor, whose flanks are stony and dark with a mantle of heather. It then descends steeply, circumventing a small pool lying in a grassy basin. The pool is curiously named Dry Mere .After passing under a line of pylons the Lydgate Bridleway is met. The O.S. maps suggest the right of way goes north along the bridleway before resuming a westerly course but in fact, it is quite acceptable to follow the well defined path which goes more directly over rolling farmland to the recently renovated cottage of Syke. Here a narrow country lane leads once more to the shores of Hollingworth Lake about three-hundred yards south of the car park or, for those who have built up a thirst, four hundred yards from a public house!

ROUTE 17
BLACKSTONE EDGE from the Windy Hill Radio Mast

Distance - 2 miles (one way) - difficult terrain

The terrible and muddy terrain of Blackstone Edge's south eastern flanks makes this ascent more suitable for hippos

The summit of Blackstone Edge

and those with masochistic tendencies than for lovers of spectacular scenery. In addition, the finest feature, those bold western cliffs,are seen only on the final stages. Yet this is one of the more famous approaches, being the one adopted by the Pennine Way. Indeed this is how I was introduced to the hill - fully laden with camping gear, tiring fast in the late afternoon sun and floundering in soggy peat,!

The G.P.O.'s Windy Hill radio mast towers above its wireless and telegraph station, which lies by the side of the A672 road. It also overlooks the busy M62 motorway linking the cities and towns of Merseyside and Greater Manchester with those of Yorkshire. Cars can be left at ref. 984144 at the start of the route. The path descends northwards to cross the motorway using the specially constructed concrete Pennine Way footbridge. A cairned path is then followed north-west-wards until a Pennine Way sign points the way northwards across grassy slopes before reaching the spongy peat terrain of the aptly named Slippery Moss. From here the route curves around to slightly descend to the watershed south of the Rishworth Drain (incorrectly shown on 1:50000 maps as continuing to Low House Moor). We are now in the midst of the horribly swampy dark peatlands of Redmires. Planks and duck-boards are used to cross the worst of the waterlogged channels but are often barely accessible themselves (as can be judged by the depths of the boot (or should I say leg-prints) from previous unfortunate travellers! Redmires has been described as the worst mile of the Pennine Way although, in my opinion, it does not rival the quagmires of Bleaklow or Featherbed Moss on the Dark Peak.

Things do improve slowly on further ascent and it does come as tremendous relief when the first gritstone crags are encountered preceding that final glorious promenade along the celebrated Blackstone Edge. Perhaps the toils are forgotten on viewing the industrial Pennine Panoramas from the firm airy summit but unfortunately it all has to be done again on the return to Windy Hill!

Blackstone Edge summit

STOODLEY PIKE

O.S.Landranger Map (1:50000) No. 103 and No. 109
or
Outdoor Leisure Map (1:25000) No. 21 'South Pennines'

Route 18 From Lumbutts
Route 19 From Charlestown
Route 20 From Blackstone Edge
Route 21 A circular from Cragg Vale

Stoodley Pike is the dominant feature on the northern edge of a tract of high moorland parcelled by the Calder Valley east of Todmorden, the Rochdale Canal and Cragg Vale. Although not the highest point of the group (that distinction fall to Little Holder Stones on Blake Moor, two miles to the south), Stoodley Pike's one-hundred and twenty two foot monument elevates it to the grandest. The monument was first built in 1815 after locals were granted permission by the landowners to commemorate the Peace of Ghent. The original monument, which looked like a mill chimney, collapsed in 1854 - said to be on the day the Russian Ambassador left London at the start of the Crimean War. The present monument was constructed in 1856 when peace was declared. It has stood firm ever since a partial collapse in November 1918, just before the end of the First World War.

Above Todmorden's tall factory chimneys and grey terraces are the pastures of Lumbutts and Mankinholes, divided into tiny fields forming an emerald mosaic, which rises to the steep northern edge of Stoodley and Langfield Common. The upper slopes and moorland's edge are embedded with crag and boulders of millstone grit, stained dark by natural oxidation and catalysed by the soot and grime from bygone industries of the Victorian times.

South of the escarpment's edge, the rolling plateau becomes rough and marshy, covered by heather and course moorland grasses. The wildness that must have seemed so complete in the past is now rudely interrupted by the scheme in which the waters from the hills are collected and channelled via concrete leats into the high level reservoirs of Warland, Light Hazzles, White Holme and Blackstone Edge. Less obtrusive in its deep moorland combe at the head of the beautiful wooded Cragg Vale, is the reservoir of Withens Clough.

There are many interesting walks to Stoodley Pike, the best known being the one along the Pennine Way from Blackstone Edge to Charleston near Hebden Bridge. All have their merits and explore different facets of the hill from the sprawling heather moors to the shapely gritstone edge: all offer remarkable views of contrasting rural and urban landscapes.

Stoodley Pike from Withens Gate

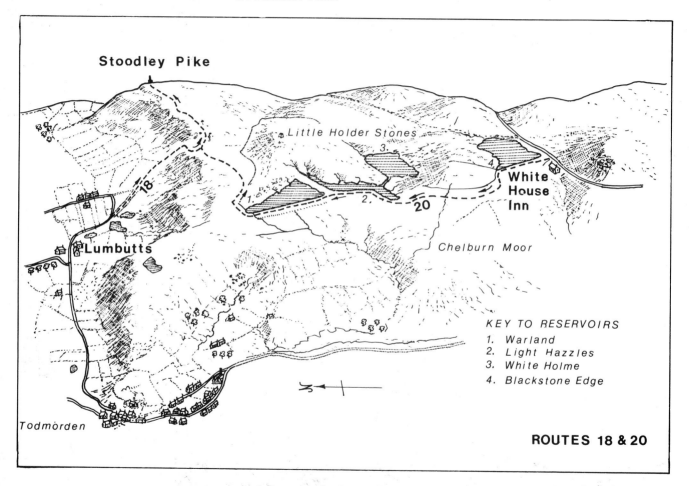

Stoodley Pike

Little Holder Stones

18

White House Inn

20

Lumbutts

Chelburn Moor

Todmorden

KEY TO RESERVOIRS
1. Warland
2. Light Hazzles
3. White Holme
4. Blackstone Edge

ROUTES 18 & 20

Stoodley Pike from the Langfield Edge

High Brown Knoll (right) & Crimsworth Dean from Slack

ROUTE 18
STOODLEY PIKE from Lumbutts

Distance 1¹/₂ miles (one way) easy

This short walk is one of the most delightful and stimulating in the area, highlighting the attractively sculpted northern flanks and with the objective, the Stoodley Pike Monument rarely out of view.

The route commences at the hamlet of Lumbutts (ref. 958233), a mile south west of Todmorden on a track which passes two small reservoirs before climbing south eastwards to the foot of Coldwell Hill's steep grassy slopes, where it meets a path from Mankinholes. Beyond the intersection, the path is constructed from gritstone paving slabs now smoothed and rounded by the elements and the pounding of heavy boots. The surface makes easy going of the stiff hill climb that follows, allowing the walker to leisurely contemplate fascinating retrospective views in which the craggy Langfield edge arcs round the plains of Lumbutts. Further afield Todmorden languishes in the Calder Valley surrounded by pale high moors of Inchfield and Rough Hill, which rise from lush pastures and hillside farms. The town from this vantage looks as clean as a whistle and fresh colour is added by the red tiled roofs of newer dwellings. In the view ahead, the uniformity of Stoodley's western facade is broken by a series of small knolls which catch the early morning light to enhance its form. It's

monument dominates but occasionally the attention is diverted to the fine looking church tower of Cross Stone perched on the hillside high above the Calder Valley and built from millstone grit, now darkened to a sooty black.

The path emerges on the summit plateau at Withens Gate. Here we leave the flagged footpath, which now descends to Withens Clough Reservoir, and follow the well trodden course of the Pennine Way tracing the escarpment's edge. What follows is an amiable stroll along a well defined and firm path lined by gritstone boulders and cotton sedge. After walking for three quarters of a mile, passing a disused quarry en route, the dark monument on the summit is reached. This impressive grimy giant can be entered from the north side, where a spiral staircase leads eerily into the darkness of its inner recesses before emerging on the viewing platform at the base of the obelisk. From here there are uninterrupted views of Calderdale and South East Lancashire.

ROUTE 19
STOODLEY PIKE from Charlestown (Calder Valley)

Distance 2 miles (one way) moderate

This ascent, which is another popular Pennine Way route, explores the hill's northern slopes. The first part of the walk is through woodland and would thus make an itinerary

Langfield Edge and the hamlets of Lumbutts and Manknholes

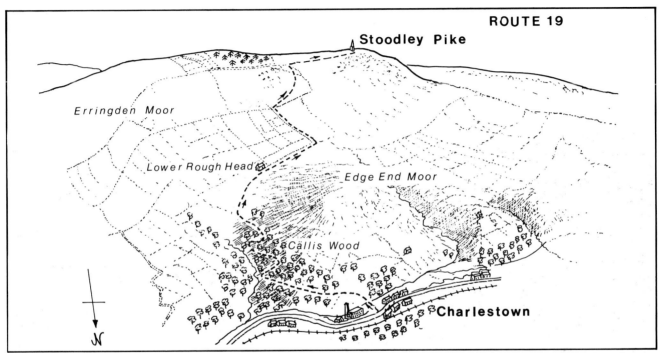

ROUTE 19

Stoodley Pike

Erringden Moor

Lower Rough Head

Edge End Moor

Callis Wood

Charlestown

N

for an Autumn day, when the abundant Hazel leaves would be at their most colourful.

Charlestown, a suburb of Hebden Bridge, lies in the narrow, steep-sided Calder Valley, through which run, the river, a railway, the A646 Halifax Road and the Rochdale Canal. The stone valleyside houses are dark from the grime exuded from the mill chimneys in bygone days when the place was a prosperous hive of activity. Now we have cheap imports and Charlestown lies dormant and slightly dog-eared in an otherwise delightful setting. The life and sound comes from the heavy motor traffic which hurries by to destinations further afield.

At ref. 972264, the walk gets an inauspicious start, passing by a sewage works before crossing the Rochdale

Canal, where highly-coloured canal boats brighten the scene. A good track zig-zags through Callis Wood, which occupies a little niche between the rounded knoll of Edge End Moor and Erringden Moor. In retrospective views, the Calder Valley seems more green, unspoiled and less grimy. It seems more peaceful - save for the now more mellow drone of the road traffic and the rhythmic rumble of passing trains.

The track emerges from the woods and passes a farmhouse at Lower Rough Head, where Stoodley Pike's monument, crowning steep grassy slopes, can now be seen across enclosed pastures. A path continues south-westwards until, at ref. 977251, it changes to a south easterly course by a dry-stone wall. A stile at a wall corner (ref. 981248) then precedes the

The monument, Stoodley Pike

climb to the ridge, which is gained to the east of the monument. A short stroll then leads to the summit where spectacular views are revealed of the Todmorden and the Calder Valley to the west.

There are many alternative return routes. The best would be to go eastwards along the high ridge, descending across Erringden Moor to the twisting narrow lane north of Erringden Grange and finally using the canalside path back to Charlestown. This would offer classic views of Britain's finest mill town, Hebden Bridge, where rows of tall Victorian stone-built terraces line the steep tree-clad valleysides beneath lofty pastures and - a landscape where urban and rural scenes amicably mingle.

ROUTE 20
STOODLEY PIKE from the White House Inn, Blackstone Edge

Distance 5 miles (one way) easy

The White House Inn lies over 1400 feet above sea level on the A58 Trans-Pennine road at the Blackstone Edge Pass high to the east above the mill town of Littleborough. The road is often the first to be closed after snow falls and this must be remembered if the walk is to be undertaken in the winter months.

The route, which follows the Pennine Way's southern approach, is one of the easiest in the book - a ridge walk without the toils of the initial ascent. It begins at ref. 969179 to the north of the inn on a gravelled Water Authority road by the Blackstone Edge Reservoir's Dam. The smooth surface of the track affords the walker a very fast pace and, if the near landscape seems artificial, then there is compensation in the fascinating and subtly changing views towards the industrial valley in the west. Bird lovers will be able to see a rich variety of species on the quiet heather moors.

A small gritstone outcrop is passed at Light Hazzles Edge before the Light Hazzles and Warland Reservoirs are encountered. At the northern tip of the latter, the road veers to the right, following the direction of a concrete leat, the Warland Drain. This channel collects water from the vast moors to the east and conveys it to the chain of reservoirs. Stoodley Pike's promontory has come into view and its monument can clearly be seen on the skyline beyond Coldwell Hill. To the west, across endless tracts of heather, a cragged fell with squarish profile catches the eye. Although the highest spot in this moorland group it's summit is unnamed. It is generally referred to as Holder Stones, the name of the rock outcrops nearby.

At ref. 964220, the track and the Warland Drain turn south east and their course is abandoned for a cairned path which heads northwards across open grassy moors to Coldwell Hill whose summit is marked by a large cairn. Views of Stoodley are now superb and seen for the first time is the Green Withens Reservoir, languishing in a huge hollow.

From Coldwell Hill, the edge of the gritstone escarpment is followed on an undulating path. The delightful and carefree stroll which follows, reveals increasingly interesting views of Todmorden and the Calder Valley en route to the zenith at Stoodley Pike.

A possible variation for the return route, although circuitous, would be to divert at ref. 965220 and follow the Warland Drain westwards across the Turley Holes and Higher House Moor and then tracing the Whiteholme Drain to its reservoir before rejoining the original path at Light Hazzles Edge. This is a Water Authority agreed courtesy path.

ROUTE 21
STOODLEY PIKE - A circular from Cragg Vale

Distance 6 miles - moderate

The village of Cragg lies peaceful and secluded in the heart of Cragg Vale to the south west of Mytholmroyd, and at the junction of the B6138 Mytholmroyd to Littleborough Road and a minor road to Withens Clough Reservoir. It is splendidly situated beneath steep wooded slopes and by the chattering Turvin Clough, which has flowed down from the bare moors of Blackstone Edge.

This superb route begins at ref.001233. by the nineteenth century church of St John the Baptist and passes the Hinchcliffe Arms. This inn has an interesting collection of coins and the equipment used by the Cragg Vale coiners, an infamous band of counterfeiters. The coiners would clip the gold from edges of Spanish and Portugese coins then put them back into circulation. They used the clippings to manufacture

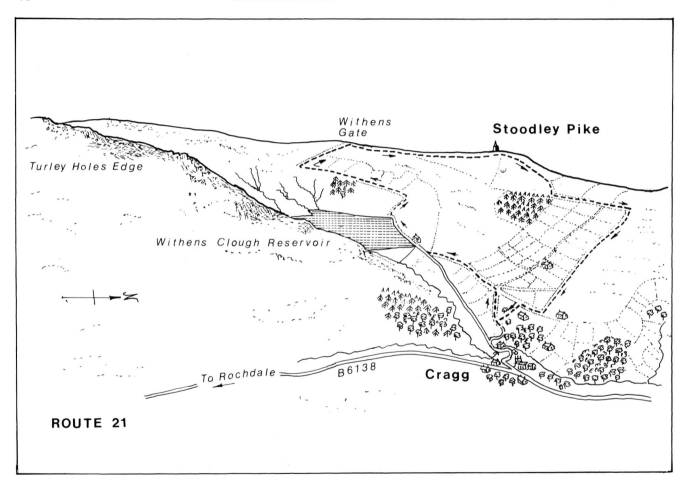

Withens
Gate

Stoodley Pike

Turley Holes Edge

Withens Clough Reservoir

To Rochdale B6138 **Cragg**

ROUTE 21

English sovereigns, which in those days were hand pressed and easy to counterfeit. Led by 'King' David Hartley of Bell House, the coiners were regarded as local heroes, but it all went wrong when a Customs and Excise man, who was hot on their trail, was found brutally murdered. David Hartley was subsequently tried, found guilty and hanged at York.

Beyond the Hinchcliffe Arms, a narrow, winding tarmac lane at ref. 998233 is used to climb the hillside to the north and away from the reservoir approach road. It becomes a stony, walled track by Swan Bank Farm (ref. 995235) and this continues westwards with views ahead of Withens Clough Reservoir and its surrounding craggy hillsides. The track descends slightly to meet the reservoir road just short of the huge earth-fill dam. The route now follows the Calderdale Way and will continue to do so until the top of the ridge at Withens Gate is reached. The reservoir's northern shores are followed on a wide track to ref.978229. Here a signposted path climbs north-westwards before turning left at a stile (ref. 977233) (not the path to the south marked as the C.W. by the 1:25000 O.S. Map.). The wall is then followed eastwards across a scruffy hillside - sadly sombre and uninvitingly derelict. The best views are the retrospective ones beyond the lake towards the fields and moors of Wadsworth at this stage. A stone wall is reached- not the usual type but a tall regular one which, with its neighbouring walls, seems to imprison the hillside. It does however guide us as we turn right (north westwards) on a walled track to the ridge. A stone on the right marked "Te deum laudmus"-we praise thee O Lord,is a sacred point on an old corpse road between Cragg and Mankinholes where bearers would rest the coffin.

After passing through a gate at the end of the track we are at last on the open fell by the remains of an old quarry, one of many on these fells. You get a feeling of elation and freedom. The best part of the walk begins here!

The path to the top of the ridge on the western edge is marked by guide stones and, in the later stages, the paving slabs, so typical of these causeways, become evident. The path meets the Pennine Way on the ridge top at Withens Gate and the Calderdale descends down the hill to Mankinholes. The view across the edge is impressive with the cliffs of Langfield Edge particularly dominant. Beneath them, in a verdant basin, are the ancient villages of Lumbutts and Mankinholes. Further afield is Todmorden distant and remote from here and dwarfed by the high moors on the opposite side of the Calder Valley.

The path from Withens Gate follows the route described in the ascent from Mankinholes but briefly this follows the edge north eastwards to the monument of Stoodley Pike which is perched high on a craggy escarpment.

From the monument, the route descends eastwards,still along the Pennine Way route, which it leaves at ref.978243 when that path turns northwards across a stile. We continue along the wall towards some newly planted conifer forest. The right of way which rakes down te slopes towards the reservoir has been obstructed by a high wall and so the best way is to turn left and follow a wide old drovers' road, known as Dick's Lane (marked as a black dotted line on 1:50000 maps).

It is possible to use the old Cragg Road by the ruin (986247) to descend Bell House Moor but it is walled and better prospects can be had by continuing to the next wall corner and descending on a parallel course (SE) guided by a dry-stone wall to the right all the way to a farm track at ref.998238. The airy views over the fields of Cragg Vale to the brown cap of Crow Hill are supplemented by those across the Mytholmroyd and the Calder Valley to the Wadsworth and Warley Moors.

After turning left at the farm track and passing above the sprawling buildings of Hill Top Farm, the route descends on a path from a gate (995237) across a field. Steps over a wall lead into a wood and out to the lane at Swan Bank Farm where steps are retraced back to Cragg village.

Stoodley Pike and Heptonstall from High Brown Knoll

HEBDEN BRIDGE'S DEANS & HILLS

O.S. Landranger Map (1:50000) No. 103 & 104
Outdoor Leisure Map (1:25000) No.21 'South Pennines'

Route 22 High Brown Knoll and Crimsworth Dean - a circular from New Bridge
Route 23 Heptonstall Moor & Hardcastle Crags - a circular from Slack

Hebden Bridge lies in Calderdale amidst steep sylvan slopes. Its stone-built Victorian four-storey terraces and old mills crowd the river and hillsides. Above are the high pastures and farmsteads that remain from communities far older than those on the valley floor. Industry is never very far away from the hills, and remains of old mines quarries, mill chimneys are all evident in lofty corners of Calderdale.

Nowadays Hebden Bridge is known for its influx of walking tourists both at weekends and bank holidays. They are lured to the Deans - Luddenden, Crimsworth, Hardcastle Crags and Cragg Vale - all very beautiful and steeped in history.

Both the routes I have included in this section walk the length of such a valley. Crimsworth Dene, with its beautiful waterfall, is visited on the walk to High Brown Knoll whilst Hardcastle Crags is included in the climb to Heptonstall Moor.

In the Stoodley Pike section there is a walk along Cragg Vale which runs westwards from Mytholmroyd.

High Brown Knoll is a fine summit with sweeping views over miles of West Yorkshire. It rises from the Crimsworth and Luddenden Deans and joins in the north a vast ridge of moorland that spans thirteen miles between Nelson in the west and Ogden north of Halifax in the east.

ROUTE 22
HIGH BROWN KNOLL & CRIMSWORTH DEAN
A Circular from New Bridge

Distance 5 miles - easy to moderate

Note. The two 1:50000 maps required (ie nos 103 and 104) will be unhelpful on this route and I strongly recommend the larger scale 'South Pennine' map.

New Bridge (map ref.989292), the chosen starting point of the walk, lies at the end of a minor road from Hebden Bridge marked 'To Hardcastle Crags'. It has a large National Trust car park and is gloriously set where the wooded Ravines of Crimsworth Dean and Hardcastle Crags (Hebden Dale) meet.

This splendid walk to High Brown Knoll is a superb combination of woodland and wild moorland with wide pano-

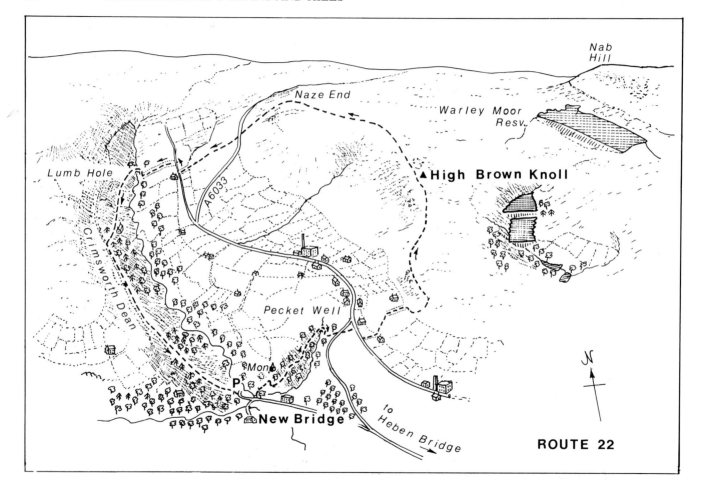

Nab Hill

Naze End

Warley Moor Resv.

Lumb Hole

A6033

▲**High Brown Knoll**

Crimsworth Dean

Pecket Well

Mon?

P

New Bridge

to Heben Bridge

N

ROUTE 22

ramas of distant hills. In the early stages to the foot of the moors, it utilizes the waymarked Calderdale Way

A track which just to the east of the public toilets is used to climb the sylvan slopes of Lower Crimsworth. Shortly, there is a choice of three paths. The middle one is taken and this circumvents the hill. High above, on the brow of the hill, is an obelisk reminiscent of that on Stoodley Pike. It is, in fact, a war memorial. After crossing a stream at Kitling Bridge (ref.994294), the path climbs out of the Dean to the village of Pecket Well, crossing ,first the A6033 road and then a minor road from Chiserley. After turning right along the minor road for a hundred yards, a Calderdale Way sign points the way eastwards on a farm track to Far Shaw Croft Farm. A path to the left of the buildings then rakes north eastwards up the hillside to ref.000293 where a walled track leads to the open fells. Here we part company from the Calderdale Way, which heads south for Wadsworth Moor. Our route follows the grassy groove of an old quarry track north eastwards to Deer Stones Edge. Just below the edge, an old ruined building and a cylindrical air shaft mark the site of a disused mine.

When the summit plateau is reached the track continues across the moor grass terrain of its western edge. Looking westwards you can see down the length of Hardcastle Crags. After the edge veers to the left below Summer Rake Edge, a sketchy path leads north-eastwards to the summit but, providing that visibility is good, the trig point will be in view and making a beeline for it presents no problems.

The views from the summit are spectacular. To the west, across the shoulder of Shackleton Moor, the rough hills of Black Hameldon and Boulsworth Hill catch the eye with the bleak Gorple and Widdop Reservoirs lying beneath their craggy slopes. Further south, on the opposite side of the Calder Valley, one's attention is immediately drawn to Stoodley Pike's monument. To its south is Blackstone Edge, in close proximity to the Windy Hill transmitter mast. Beyond, amongst the peaks of Derbyshire, Black Hill is particularly dominant. In the east, across pale grassy moors, a high sheet of water, the Warley Moor Reservoir languishes below, Nab Hill, a crag interspersed escarpment. The two closer Dean Reservoirs are hidden from view by High Brown Knoll's concave eastern slopes.

From the summit, the cairned Limers' Gate track leads north westwards across the summit plateau to Naze End before descending to the A6033 road. We are now overlooking the beautiful Crimsworth Dean which will guide us back to New Bridge. Just to the south ,along the road, a metal post indistinctly marks the start of a footpath, which descends westwards to meet a small gate lying secluded in a hollow to the right of two five-barred gates marked 'private'. After going through the small gate, a narrow footpath between fences then leads to a country lane at ref. 995312. This was once the main Hebden Bridge to Haworth road and ,although navigable on foot, is metalled only to Gram Water Bridge one mile to the north.

Turn right along the road for a hundred yards before turning left along a paved path which goes down to the banks of Crimsworth Dean Beck. Hereabouts in a beautiful wooded niche are the Lumb Hole Waterfalls close to a splendid old

Lumb Hole waterfall, Crimsworth Dean

stone pack-horse bridge. The bridge is crossed and the track doubles back climbing the opposite banks. By two stone gateposts the track is left for a footpath,which traverses fields high above the beck. The prospect is an extremely beautiful one with woodlands of pine, birch, and oak, mingling with verdant pastures fringed by high moorland tops. The river gurgles and ,more often than not, the sound of birdsong echoes through the valley. Beyond a rustic cottage, the path climbs through a copse of pine to meet a high cart track which passes through mixed woodland and runs the length of the Dean to reach the car park at New Bridge. It is an easy paced end to a beautiful walk.

ROUTE 23
HEPTONSTALL MOOR
- a Circular from Slack via Hardcastle Crags

Distance 5¹/₂ miles- moderate

This walk starts at the National Trust car park on the old Hebden Bridge to Nelson road at ref.969298, north of the hillside village of Slack. The car park overlooks the popular valley of Hardcastle Crags and is in the shade of Heptonstall Moor.

A stony track descends eastwards by a lively stream down the valleyslopes of Hardcastle Crags. At the first junction of tracks the left one is taken and this in turn is abandoned for gritstone steps,which lead directly to a bridge over Hebden

Water adjacent to Gibson Mill .

After circumventing the mill, a wide track is then taken westwards, passing the old mill pond and weir in a glorious woodland setting. The track gradually climbs to some large outcrops of millstone grit, which presumably are the Hardcastle Crags giving the valley its name. Beyond the crags, there is a fork in the tracks. The left one is taken. Through the trees the river can be seen below tumbling over another weir. Close by a footbridge spans its waters. Our track continues along the valleyside and leads out of the woods where a cascading waterfall tumbles from the slopes of Wadsworth Moor to the river below. By the waterfall is the charming rustic cottage of Overwood.

The path procedes, high on the grassy slopes of Black Dean where there are remains of old quarries and a network of tramways. The remains of an old ruined railway bridge span the river below. This was part of a railway built to supply materials for the construction of the Walshaw Dean Reservoirs. In the view ahead the valley is divided by a craggy, partially wooded spur, known as the Ridge (not named on 1:50000 maps). Alcomden Water and Graining Water meet at its foot and each is spanned by a bridge, the former for travellers on foot and the latter conveys the old road between Hebden Bridge and Nelson. Further distant beyond the crags of Ridge Scout above Graining Water are the spartan moors of Heptonstall and Widdop. Dusky heather, dark gritstone and pale moor grasses merge on the slopes in a dappled mosaic of muted colour.

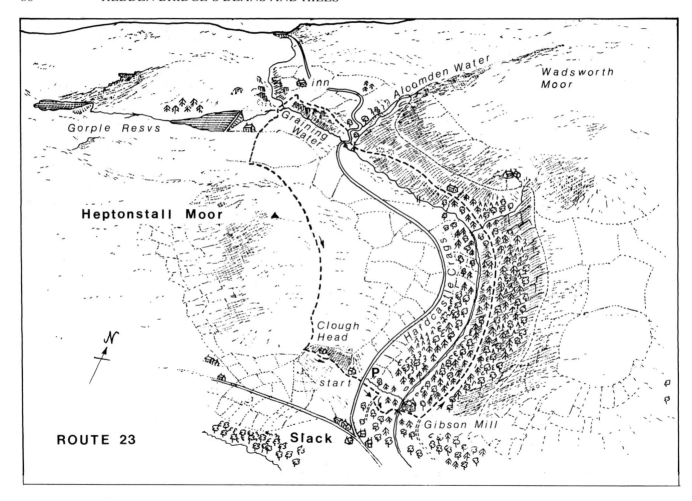

Gorple Resvs

inn

Aloamden Water

Wadsworth Moor

Graining Water

Heptonstall Moor

Hardcastle Crags

N

Clough Head

start

P

Gibson Mill

ROUTE 23

Slack

A descent is made to the footbridge over Alcomden Water, where the path climbs to a gate onto a Water Board road, which then exits onto the Nelson Lane. After turning right to climb the lane to the next bend, it is left for a footpath which then continues westwards across crag-ridden, grassy slopes above the bluffs of Ridge Scout.

Opposite to the huge grass banks of Lower Gorple Reservoir's earth-fill dam, two little wooden foot-bridges can be seen spanning Graining Water and an outflow of the lake. We will have to cross these later, but first the path continues northwards to ref. 948317 where the flagged Pennine Way track is met. The route follows the Pennine Way for the next two miles across Heptonstall Moor. The white building to the east is the Pack Horse Inn and those with a thirst could well take a break here.

The Pennine Way path is taken down to the river, where it crosses the two previously mentioned bridges before climbing the steep grassy banks beneath the Reservoir's dam. The paving slabs are evident once more, as the brow of the bank is reached. Preceding the open moor, the Gorple Cottages belonging to the Water Authority are passed. In the sixties, a former keeper was tragically killed in blizzard conditions - a reminder that hills can be harsh places for the inexperienced.

Beyond the cottages and some tall iron gates, a leat is crossed. A wide track then leads southwards climbing the northern slopes of Heptonstall Moor. On reaching a fence, the track is abandoned. A path then follows the southern side of the fence until the point when it veers ENE. The cairned path maintains its direction ESE across Heptonstall Moor. For those who like to reach a definite summit, a trig point which crowns Standing Stone Hill, the highest point, is a simple but trackless stroll to the right (not advisable however in poor visibility.) Views to the north and east are wide and airy. They encompass a sweep of high moorland including Boulsworth Hill, Withins Height, Wadsworth Moor and High Brown Knoll. We are just high enough to see the Walshaw Dean Reservoirs beneath the heather-clad Withins Height and cradled between the spurs of Wadsworth and Widdop Moors. As the path descends over the shoulder of Clough Head Hill Heptonstall village comes into view, its fine church perched proudly on lofty, green walled pastures. Beyond it and across the Calder Valley, Stoodley Pike re-appears on the horizon.

The eastern edge of the moor is reached at Clough Head and we find ourselves looking down a rugged ravine to more gentle pastures. Shackleton Moor and High Brown Knoll ahead are cut deep by the curving, wooded valleys of Hardcastle Crags and Crimsworth Dean.

Closer at hand, you should also be able to pick out the car park at the start of the walk and we have to descend the clough to get back down there. After going through the gate in the wall that circumvents the ravine, a narrow path traverses lush grass slopes to pass behind the ruins of a grand old farmhouse. A prominent track then descends in magnificent verdant pastoral scenery past the occupied farmhouse of Clough House to meet the road directly opposite to the National Trust car park and starting point of the walk.

INCHFIELD MOOR

> O.S. Landranger Map (1:50000) No. 103
> Outdoor Leisure Map (1:25000) No. 21 'South Pennines'
>
> Route 24 A Circular from Gorpley Clough Foot

Inchfield Moor is, at 1488 feet (454 metres), the highest of the hills that surround Todmorden. The summit, known as Freeholds Top, is the zenith in the central regions of a moorland mass rising from Rochdale in the south and declining to Burnley in the north. As a viewing platform it is superb, giving wide vistas of the Rossendale and Calder Valleys, Stoodley Pike and Blackstone Edge. As a fell in its own rights, Inchfield disappoints, for there is a lack of true character or recognisable form; no crags to speak of and the ridge is usually far too waterlogged for free-striding except to the south where things really do improve.

Ramsden Clough and Gorpley Clough bite deep into Inchfield's eastern slopes. Both are lovely but have been savaged in their upper reaches by small reservoirs which bear their name. A row of electricity pylons dissects the marshy eastern moors below the reservoirs' dams and several decaying farm dwellings add desolation to the area. However, in summer when the white buds of the cotton grass blow in the breeze, the lower slopes offer truly magnificent landscapes, enhanced by the easily recognisable backdrop of Stoodley Pike.

The western slopes of Inchfield descend to the industrial Spodden Valley, known for its sandstone quarries. The horrible tawny scars of these activities is seen on Middle Hill to the south and influenced me against including a route from Broadley, near Rochdale to Bacup via Brown Wardle Hill, Hades Hill and Inchfield Moor.

To the south of Ramsden Clough is Rough Hill, a finer place altogether: it has firm terrain and good views especially of Rochdale and Greater Manchester across the Watergrove Reservoir.

In conclusion, although I have been a little tough on Inchfield Moor, I still think it is worth including by all who wish to discover the South Pennines, for it gives different perspectives on other more favoured fells.

ROUTE 24
INCHFIELD MOOR - A Circular from Gorpley Clough Foot

Distance 7^1/$_2$ miles - moderate to hard

One mile west of Todmorden on the A681 Bacup Road (ref. 918237), the wooded glen of Gorpley Clough cuts deep into the grassy flanks of Inchfield Moor. A very obvious path,

Across Inchfield Pasture looking towards Stoodley Pike

Thieveley Scout

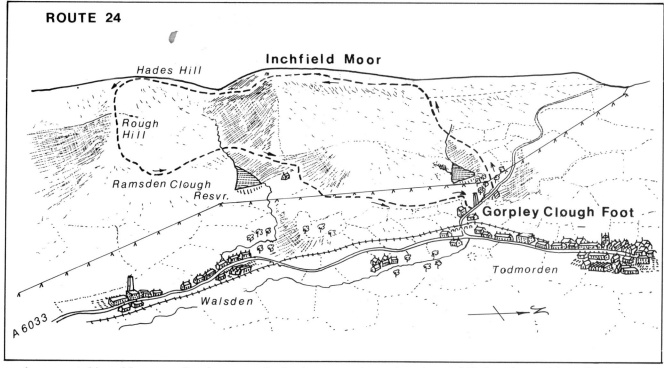

ROUTE 24

Hades Hill

Inchfield Moor

Rough Hill

Ramsden Clough Resvr.

Gorpley Clough Foot

Todmorden

Walsden

A 6033

newly renovated by a Manpower Services team, leads along the banks of the busy stream but this is not the best way to the summit. The route I chose is obscure initially and runs parallel to the road for a few yards before zig-zagging up a steep wooded spur to the north of the clough. It emerges on the high pastures to the east of Gorpley Farm and gives interesting retrospective views of Todmorden and Langfield Common beyond. After passing to the south of the farm ,a walled track is followed until it veers left descending to another farm. At this point the path maintains its direction heading towards the open moors. To the south the waters of the Gorpley Reservoir, built to supply Todmorden, lie under the steep green lower slopes of Inchfield Moor. The scene in this direction is uninspiring and marred by the line of huge electricity pylons and the reservoir's dam.

The next section of the walk is the worst, for it passes through rough open pastureland which has been deeply rutted by the hooves of the cows which frequently graze here. Things do improve however beyond the crossing of the infant Gorpley stream and, although the route to the ridge is trackless, it is fairly dry and easy to negotiate. Just prior to reaching the ridge, a cinder track leading to some disused mine-workings is crossed.

The ridge is wide and views from the middle are restricted to distant hilltops. They improve slightly just to the north west of Freeholds Top when the ridge narrows. In views to the west over the Rossendale Valley, the busy industrial towns of Bacup and Rawtenstall can be seen surrounded by high hills. Notable amongst these is Cowpe Moss, which has been defiled by vast quarries and mines and yet still retains some character and nobility. The path continues to Freeholds Top, identified by its concrete trig point and shallow circular pool around which cotton grass grows in profusion - a pleasing sight in summer months. Eastern panoramas include Langfield Common and its shapely escarpment of Stoodley Pike, easily distinguishable by its tall monument. We are also just high enough to see the Warland and Light Hazzles Reservoirs on the high and flat Langfield plateau leading the eye to the squarish profile of Little Holder Stones and, further south, the serrated craggy summit of Blackstone Edge. In the opposite direction are the less inspiring views of the Spodden Valley,

disfigured by yet more quarrying. Incidentally the River Spodden has its source not half a mile distant on Inchfield's western flanks.

It is possible to descend directly westwards from the summit but a better way is to continue along the ridge towards Hades Hill. It will be noted that no rights of way exist southwards from the summit but the routes are regularly used and no fences or walls bar the way. As the path descends, the Ramsden Clough Reservoir comes into view. There is a sense of spaciousness in this vicinity and it is accentuated by the sweeping curves of grassy hillsides. There is a slight climb to Hades Hill with views of the horribly mutilated Middle Hill, crowned by J.C.B. diggers and with brown clay quarrying scars, the scene resembles one of a huge fell-top building site! The view is quickly forgotten on the trackless climb eastwards to Rough Hill, whose summit has a gravel surface and stone cairn. The views have now opened up southwards to reach panoramic proportions. They include the vast plains where the high rise buildings of Rochdale guide the eye to the more distant cityscapes of Manchester. Beyond the plains to the south east are the pale Pennine moors of Saddleworth and the High Peak. To the north, the bare grassy slopes of Inchfield are broken by the ruined dwellings which echo the plight of the upland farmer in modern times of mechanisation. A slight detour to the south of Rough Hill would reveal the expansive Watergrove Reservoir, much frequented by the enthusiasts of water-sports. At the weekend there are usually speed-boats and yachts scurrying across its waters.

East of Rough Hill's summit, the route joins a well

defined track, which circumvents its eastern slopes, before descending by an unnamed clough to meet Ramsden Clough, which is forded at ref. 910209, to the south west of its reservoir. After climbing the northern banks, the path crosses into a field via a small ladder stile, and heads in the direction of a large ruin, Coolam (not named on 1:50000 maps). It then veers north-eastwards on a reedy track which passes more ruins high above the Ramsden Clough Reservoir. After passing under electricity pylons the track veers to the right and it is abandoned to cross ENE over the Inchfield Pasture (again not named on 1:50000 maps!). This high moorland plateau to the east of Inchfield's two reservoirs is covered with cottongrass which, when flowering, superbly decorates the day's most spectacular view. This encompasses Stoodley Pike, now boldly fronted with the cliffs of Langfield Edge. Opposite to them, the barren gritstone ridge of Black Hameldon overlooks the pleasant high hamlets of Cross Stone and Hole Bottoms which lie on a verdant shelf above the chequered fields of the Calder Valley.

At ref. 923223, just before a stream crossing, an old track, paved in places by slabs of millstone grit, is followed across lofty fields before meeting a farm track. As it descends the valleysides, the houses, factories, viaducts, railway and canal of Todmorden gradually appear in a fascinating tapestry of both rural and urban landscape.

Ahead (north), the pointed escarpment of Todmorden Moor looks appealing. Beyond the last farm, Hollow Dene, a narrow tarmac lane descends in zig-zags emerging from behind an old mill and tall brick chimney to the Bacup Road just a couple of hundred yards south east from the starting point.

Inchfield Moor

THIEVELEY PIKE

O.S. Landranger Map (1:50000) No. 103 or
Outdoor Leisure Map (1:25000) No.21 'South Pennines'

Route 25 Circular from Holme Chapel

Anyone travelling on the A646 road between Burnley and Todmorden cannot but marvel at the magnificent cliffs and screes passed at the Cliviger Gorge. These form the north-eastern facade of Thieveley Pike and are known collectively as Thieveley Scout. They are made more impressive by the foreground of verdant meadows and fine stands of broad-leafed trees. The area is a complex result of glaciation and includes limestone deposited from the Craven Area of Yorkshire in the last ice age, seams of coal, and also millstone grit which forms the broken cliffs of the Scout.

The southern slopes, known as Deerplay Moor, decline in shallow gradients and scrubby fields to the head of the River Irwell, which is born on this fell at Irwell Spring. The Burnley to Bacup main road climbs high up the hill's western slopes before descending into the Rossendale Valley.

On the summit of Thieveley is one of a series of northern beacons where fires were lit to convey important news and historic events. Its position in the chain was between Pendle Hill and Blackstone Edge. Thieveley Pike's summit plateau is spoiled in places by the traces of past industry. An old hard-core track, cairns of brick, not stone plus remains of coal and lead mines all scar the hillside, but in it favour, it offers fine unrestricted views of the hills and industrial plains of Lancashire and West Yorkshire.

A quick route from the Deerplay Inn, high on the Burnley to Bacup road, is possible but this would omit all that is best for this side of the hill is drab and uninteresting. I have chosen one circular route based on Holme Chapel, a village at the northern extremities of the Cliviger Gorge. This will, if undertaken in good weather, reveal all the delights of Thieveley and would be particularly attractive in autumn when the forests would be a blaze of colour.

ROUTE 25
THIEVELEY PIKE - A Circular from Holme Chapel

Distance 5 miles (return by road) or 6 miles via Black Scout - moderate to hard.

This eastern approach route explores all that is best of Thieveley Pike and omits much of the industrial scarring seen on the western side. It begins from ref. 877284, a couple of hundred yards to the south of Holme Chapel village, situated

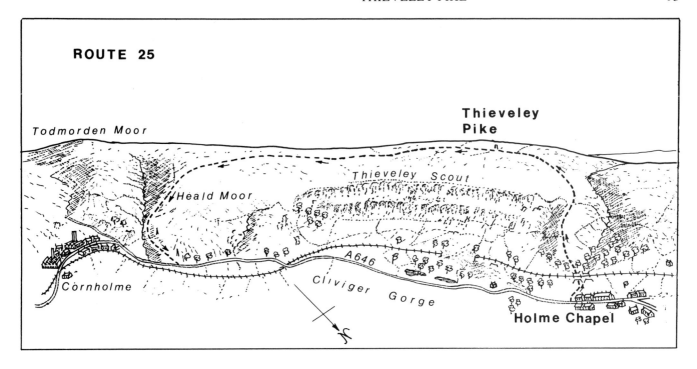

ROUTE 25

Todmorden Moor

Heald Moor

Thieveley Pike

Thieveley Scout

A 646

Cliviger Gorge

Cornholme

Holme Chapel

at the northern end of the Cliviger Gorge on the A 646 Burnley to Todmorden road. Cars can be left in the village or on a lay-by one hundred yards south of the starting point.

From the main road, the path traverses a field south westwards to the right of a stand of proud, tall ash trees before joining a walled farm-track which goes under a railway tunnel close to the place where the old Holme Chapel station would have been sited. The zig zag path then enters a dusky area of woodland and dark moss covered rocks. Black Clough to the right is aptly named and has been polluted ever since the mine, Black Clough Colliery was opened a century ago.

The next section of the walk is a delightful climb out of

the valley giving ever-widening views across the industrial East Lancashire Plains towards Pendle Hill. A narrow path leaves the farm track and winds through Buckley Wood (only marked on 1:25000 maps) giving glimpses of Pendle's 'Big End'.

On reaching the open Fell, the best route follows a right of way SSW past the remains of Thieveley Farm demolished in the thirties. In its hey day this was a popular Bank Holiday venue for the weavers of Burnley and Nelson who would have caught the train to Holme Chapel and walked up the hill. The entertainment would have been provided by hand-cranked roundabouts and swing-boats. Cricket matches were also played here! Further back in time, Robert Hartley, who farmed here, discovered a vein of lead ore which was mined, first by Mr. Hartley then by King Charles 1st. The slag heap can still be seen to the north west of the farm.

Beyond the old farm, pass through gateposts to the right of a deep clough making a beeline for the prominent gritstone outcrop (Dean Scout) at its head. From Dean Scout, across the clough's tightly enclosed ravine you can look over the prominent and precipitous millstone grit cliffs forming the fringe of Thieveley Scout. From the cliffs, the eye is led directly to Stoodley Pike, its monument standing guard above the Calder Valley towns which, from this vantage, are hidden from view by lower slopes.

In the final pull to the summit, the route traverses an area of disused opencast workings. Drainage ditches and a flinted track running above and parallel to the 'Scout' point to possible increased forestry activity in the area. (I hope I am wrong!).

Thieveley's summit is a dull place. Its trig point lies next to a barbed-wire fence and brick cairns serve as additional evidence that this is an urban hill, a point obscured on eastern ascents. In new views south-westwards, the Deerplay Moor descends to the head of the Irwell Valley. At the edge of the moorland is the Deerplay Inn just to the north of the village of Weir. Further down the valley is the larger town of Bacup, sheltered by the slopes of Cowpe Moss. The view is savaged by a line of electricity pylons, however and one seeks solace elsewhere. (Why can they not put these services underground? They might not even be so prone to damage by storms!) Prospects in other directions however are brighter. To the south lies the escarpment of Pendle Hill towering over the industrial conurbations of Burnley, Nelson and Colne. Beyond, over the rolling pastures between the River Ribble and Aire, lie the Craven Hills of Yorkshire, dominated by the instantly recognisable profiles of Ingleborough and Pen-y-Ghent. To the north east are the hills of Black Hameldon and Boulsworth Hill ,wide and wild with sparse, dark gritstone outcrops and small reservoirs - blue pools in an ochre sea of moorland grasses, interspersed with dark, peaty runnels. High on these bare hills is a white cottage, the Stiperden Bar House. It is actually on a narrow lane known as the Long Causeway but from here it looks very much isolated. Stoodley Pike captures centre-stage in views to the south, as it will for much of the trek across the ridge.

From Thieveley's summit the horrible barbed-wire fence is crossed via a stile and thankfully left far behind on a south-easterly course along a rough grassy ridge to Heald Moor. The prospects are now less dreary and the urban blues are gone; we are on top of the world and can stride carefree! Heald Moor, at the southern edge of the ridge, is marked by a leaning wooden stake. From it views of the Calder Valley have been added to the landscape. Beneath the steep eastern slopes of Carr and Crags Moor is Cornholme, a collection of terraced-houses bordering the railway track which curves gently around a large mill and factories.

A right of way exists ENE from Heald Moor and this is used to descend the rough, grassy slopes to meet a track terminating at a ruined building, ref. 894265. A sketchy northbound path then keeps to the right of a fence before entering a small forest. It then descends steeply to the A646 road at ref. 892269. Adjacent are some really impressive waterfalls which plummet down Ratten Clough, a wooded ravine beneath some high, dark crags.

By the busy road it is about one and a half miles to the starting point of the walk. A preferable return route would be to climb Black Scout (the hill on the opposite side of the road) via Dean Farm before descending to Holme Chapel via the woods above Holme House. Either way you would see the magnificent glaciated cliffs of Thieveley Scout towering above roadside pastures!

Ratten Clough Waterfalls, Portsmouth, Calder Valley

Portsmouth in the Calder Valley beneath Carr and Craggs and Heald Moors

BOULSWORTH HILL & WITHINS HEIGHT

O.S. Landranger Map (1:50000) No. 103 or
Outdoor Leisure Map (1:25000) No. 21 'South Pennines'

Route 26 Boulsworth Hill from Wycoller
Route 27 Boulsworth Hill from Coldwell Reservoirs
Route 28 Withins Height from Ponden Resvr. Haworth

Boulsworth Hill, which at 1699 feet, is the loftiest peak in the whole of the South Pennines, is part of a vast, scarcely populated tract of high moorland between the bustling towns of Colne, Haworth, Todmorden and Hebden Bridge. Like many of its neighbouring fells, it has been surrounded by small reservoirs built to serve these industrial centres.

Looking on the 1;50000 map, it would seem that the hill is purely a grassy one with few features but this is not the case and I would recommend the use of 1;25000 maps which names and shows the position of the many crags and outcrops that exist.

Boulsworth was, until recently, out of bounds to walkers and was the subject of a 'mass trespass' by the Ramblers' Association. As a result of negotiations with the Water Board, two concessionary routes have been agreed. Both ascend the northern slopes and have since been included as alternative routes in the Pendle Way Long Distance footpath. It is a pity that approaches from the west and south have been omitted but perhaps, with further persuasion the newly privatised boards will agree to add them at a later date.

The main ridge runs quite straight in a NE-SW direction. The summit is known as Lad Law and its trig. point is set amongst gritstone outcrops. A feature of the ridge is the profuse covering of cotton sedge, which flecks the hills with white in summer. The Weather Stones and the Chaucer Stones lie further east but more impressive are the Dove Stones, which jut out from a southern spur, separated from the main ridge by the depression cut by Heys Slacks Clough. These gigantic angular buttresses and slabs are made very distinctive by one detached and crooked obelisk. The spur comes to an abrupt end where the steep craggy fellsides plunge to the huge hollow of the Widdop Reservoir.

Boulsworth's southern slopes are vast and drained by a complex series of streams and cloughs. The principle ones are Greave Clough, which flows south through the heather-clad grouse moors of Widdop and Heather Hill, and also to its east, Walshaw Dean. This river begins life on the mosses of Jackson's Ridge to cut a wide valley amongst barren peaty hillslopes. It is then dammed to form the three Walshaw Dean Reservoirs before flowing as Alcomden Water into Graining water, north west of Hardcastle Crags.

Boulsworth's wild north-western flanks are steep, grassy and, on the whole, featureless. Under them the old town of Trawden reposes, strangely isolated from the rest of East Lancashire's industrial belt. To the north, dark heathery slopes decline to the Water Sheddles Reservoir, lying by the Colne to Haworth road on a wild high pass.

Withins Height overlooks the valley of Walshaw Dean and is part of a five mile NW-SE ridge connecting Boulsworth's north eastern outlier, Crow Hill to Oxenhope Moor. Withins Height is visited on the Pennine Way and has largely been made famous by its connections with the Brontë Family for both Ponden Hall, at its foot, and Top Withens, close to the summit, are said to have inspired locations for Emily's 'Wuthering Heights'.

The hill has two distinct sides to its character. Its featureless south western sides, which rise from the Walshaw Dean Reservoirs are rough, peaty and heather-clad whilst the north-eastern face is grassy and, although still stark and dramatically desolate, this side of the hill has been sculpted better by more shapely ravines cut by Ponden Clough and South Dean. The hill offers good views of nearby Haworth and the verdant Worth Valley. Although not a spectacular place, it does have a certain charm on a good day.

ROUTE 26
BOULSWORTH HILL from Wycoller

Distance 3¹/₂ miles (one way) - moderate with steep finale

This is Boulsworth's most rewarding ascent and many may feel that the initial rambles through Wycoller Dean are superior to the harsher moorland walking closer to the summit.

Wycoller once thrived on the exploits of both farming and weaving but, during the industrial revolution, the mill factories of the bigger towns such as Colne and Burnley took over. The Water Authorities purchased the village with the intention of flooding the valley to form a new reservoir, but the scheme was never commenced. In the 1940's, the 'Friends of Wycoller' restored the site and, in 1973, the Lancashire County Council bought much of the area and turned it into a delightful country park.

The best place to leave a vehicle is on the official car park (ref. 937394) just off the Colne to Haworth road and a quarter of a mile to the east of Wycoller village centre. A steep descent is then made across fields into the dean, reaching the ruins of Wycoller Hall, once the home of the powerful Cunliffe family. It is said that Charlotte Brontë based her Ferndean Manor from 'Jane Eyre' on this dwelling. By the hall flows a shallow stream, forded by a rough metalled track. Close by is a pack-horse bridge as fine as any I have seen and set amongst trees and charming stone cottages. In Spring the colourful daffodils add further splendour to the scene.

A narrow metalled lane, which follows the stream's banks south-eastwards from the hall, leads past two more primitive stone bridges as it threads through the tree-lined dean. High on the fellsides to the west are a couple of typical northern hill farms, looking as stark and romantic as anything from a Brontë novel. At ref. 937388 there is confusion as many signposted paths, unmarked on the present O.S. map con-

The pack-horse bridge, Wycoller

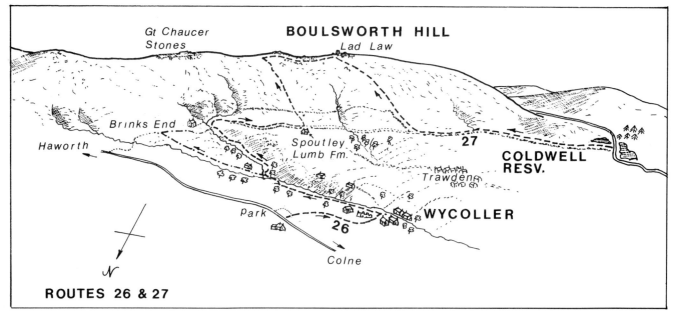

ROUTES 26 & 27

verge. Two are usable, meeting once more at ref. 941379 west of Brinks End Farm. The first follows a route used by the Pendle and Brontë Way long distance footpaths. It continues along the dilapidated tarmac lane to the farmhouse of Parson Lee where a track, which can be muddy, climbs to and traverses high green fields before meeting another marshy track. This leads south-westwards to Brinks End. A more interesting alternative follows a courtesy path signposted 'To Trawden'. This crosses Wycoller Beck and follows its tribu-tary on a well defined, if devious, path through Turnhole Clough, a delightful narrow wooded glen leading to the west of Brinks End. The path, which follows the stream's western banks, passes over, in its later stages, some wild bracken-clad open moorland. Boulsworth's enticing slopes figure in the view ahead, whilst isolated gritstone crags crown grassy slopes to the west of the clough with the farm of Brinks End, high on its opposite flanks. The two routes converge to the west of the farm when the former descends and crosses

Turnhole Clough to join the latter. It is now evident that we are on a very prominent ancient road, which is paved with slabs of millstone grit. Streams from the high moorland descend to meet Turnhole Clough in a triangular, steep-banked basin which forms the foreground of a very wild barren landscape. High on the horizon, the Chaucer Stones add a little shape to the otherwise smooth profiles of Boulsworth's ridge. It would be very tempting to head for this high ground even though it would involve trespass but, in this case, the official route is best. The ascent begins by the lonely farm of Spoutley Lumb (ref. 927369) on a concrete Water Authority road which leads to a small reservoir. From here, a waymarked path rises steeply on the concave peaty slopes of Pot Brinks Moor with the objective out of view until the very last stage.

A few small gritstone outcrops (The Little Chair Stones) are seen on attaining the ridge. The succeeding walk past the

Dove Stones

Weather Stones to the summit of Lad Law is now easy stuff, although it can be a trifle marshy after periods of rain. The summit is furnished with a concrete trig. point set close to gritstone crags, which offer much shelter from the elements and also good perches to consume lunch in relative comfort. Striking views are revealed over the East Lancashire industrial towns to the whaleback of Pendle Hill and, further afield, to Pen-y-Ghent and Ingleborough. To the south, the sculpted crags of Dove Stones beckon like a magnet and, although it is unofficial, I think a detour across the wet cotton-sedge moors that lie between would be well worth the minimal effort involved.

A possible return route to Wycoller would be to descend directly from Lad Law down Bedding Hill Moor and Gilford Clough to the village of Trawden, then cutting across to Wycoller either by country lane or by following one of the many farmland paths. No extra time or mileage would be incurred.

ROUTE 27
BOULSWORTH HILL from the Coldwell Reservoirs near Nelson

Distance - 2¹/₂ miles(one way) - easy but with steep finale

This is the least interesting but offers the quickest legal approach to Boulsworth's summit - suitable for a Summer evening or short afternoon walk.

It begins at ref. 903362 at a gate, which interrupts the

high castellated stone walls obscuring the Coldwell Reservoirs from motorists passing along the road between Nelson and Hebden Bridge. An eastbound cart track ascends gradually to the lofty fields of Will Moor, with retrospective views to Pendle Hill beating those of Boulsworth ahead. The track descends slightly to cross Will Moor Clough before being abandoned at ref. 921366 for a signposted courtesy path climbing south eastwards over the steep grassy inclines of Bedding Hill Moor. In views to the north, the scene is pastoral with the fields of Trawden stretching to the Colne Valley far below.

After being guided by a dry-stone wall in the early stages, the path maintains its direction on the open fell to reach the Abbot's Stone, first of a series of gritstone slabs. The steep slopes relent as the summit is neared and, for the first time southern vistas are revealed across the sprawling grassy moors.

ROUTE 28
WITHINS HEIGHT from the Ponden Reservoir

Distance- 2¹/₂ miles (one way) - moderate

Ponden Reservoir, in the Worth Valley, is a haven for boat enthusiasts who sail on her waters. It lies amongst sleepy verdant hillslopes whose contours have been accentuated by the dark gritstone walls which clamber to austere farmhouses and the high moors above. In the valley, the main sounds come

from the frequent cars speeding by on the Colne to Haworth road.

This popular walk, which is part of the Pennine way, begins at ref. 987375 by the western shores of the reservoir on a farm track leaving the Haworth road to climb amongst high pastures. There are good views eastwards down the valley towards the village of Stanbury. The track then veers eastwards and descends to the shores of the reservoir by Ponden Hall. This fine mansion, proudly constructed from local stone, was believed to have been on Emily Bronte's mind when she

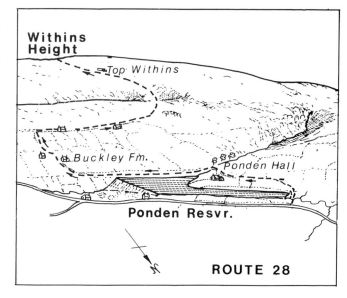

Top Withins, Withins Height

described Thrushcroft Grange in her novel, 'Wuthering Heights'.

The steep craggy combe of Ponden Clough, to the south west, looks really impressive from this angle and it is a shame that its numerous paths do not lead to the high ridge for it would make a superb approach. At the southern end of the reservoir's dam, a path, enclosed by dry-stone walls, ascends southwards past Buckley Farm to ref. 998367. Here we abandon the track for an eastbound one, which climbs to the open fellsides, passing two more loftily situated farms (Lower and Upper Heights) en route. Views across the moors of Yorkshire are now becoming quite expansive and interesting. Looking northwards across the wide pale green moorlands, the eye is led down the Worth Valley in the direction of the village of Haworth, just hidden by concave lower slopes. Haworth's vicarage was the celebrated home of the Brontë sisters, their brother and father. Further afield are the still more palid profiles of Rombalds Moor. As more height is gained, the lonely ruin of Top Withins comes into view across empty moors. It can be reached very quickly on the easy gradients of a good firm path. Another well-frequented track is seen climbing along South Dean Clough to the east. Many pilgrims each day follow this line from Haworth to Top Withins and seem unperturbed by the sign on its far wall.

It reads:-

"....This farmhouse has been associated with 'Wuthering Heights', the Earnshaw home in Emily Brontë's novel. The building, even when complete, bore no resemblance to the house she described but the situation may have been in her mind when she wrote of the moorland setting of the heights...."

The old farm is, in fact, quite small although well constructed in stone. In poor weather when the mountain mists swirl, two closely situated dwarfed and wind bent trees add to the eeriness of the place.

Beyond the ruin, the expansive plateau may be a disappointment for no new vistas are added except for the tops of Heptonstall Moor and Black Hameldon, which have little charisma from this vantage or distance. If transport is available it would be a good idea to continue along the Pennine Way and descend by the Walshaw Dean Reservoirs to the Widdop Reservoir (parking near the dam). Had it been a legal path, the finest return route would be to go north westwards along the ridge from Withins Height to Crow Hill and then descend into Ponden Clough, where rights of way then lead back to the Ponden Reservoir. Those magic words 'grouse butts' dispel any idea that this will ever be legalised.

The Hare Stones – looking towards Gorple Stones

Foster's Leap. Boulsworth Hill in the background

BLACK HAMELDON

O.S. Landranger Map (1:50000) No.103 or
Outdoor Leisure Map (1:25000) No. 21 'South Pennines'

Route 29 from Mereclough
Route 30 from Todmorden
Route 31 from Widdop Reservoir

Black Hameldon is at the heart of the lofty expanse of wild and lonely moorland rising from green farm fields and tall factory chimneys of the Calder Valley. Its summit is five miles to the east of Burnley and three and a half to the north-east of Todmorden. Black Hameldon's very name conjures up images of a dark satanic place. Indeed, on a sunless day, when its peaty upper slopes were at their blackest, the reputation would appear deserved.

The remoteness of the hill is lessened only slightly by the construction of the Gorple and Cant Clough Reservoirs, which bask in austere hollows beneath its north and west flanks respectively. Dark flinty gritstone rocks decorate approaches from the north. The finest of these are the Gorple Stones, the rocky diadem of Black Moor, and also those on Shuttleworth Moor, overlooking the dam of Gorple Upper Reservoir.

The official summit, Hoof Stones Height, lies to the south of a broad marshy ridge, which is just over a mile in length. Marked by a concrete trig point and surrounded by shallow pools, the summit is a grand place to view the distant but impressive Pendle Hill, which soars above the chimneys of Padiham, and Burnley.

Although it is a little known fell, Black Hameldon has much to offer lovers of solitude and harsh, dramatic scenery. In my opinion, the walk from Widdop Reservoir is one of this book's most splendid routes!

ROUTE 29
BLACK HAMELDON from Mereclough via Cant Clough Reservoir

Distance 4 miles (one way) moderate

Mereclough, a small hillside hamlet, is situated at the north western end of the ancient 'Long Causeway' (now a metalled lane). Although only two miles from Burnley, its altitude separates and alienates it from the East Lancashire urban scene.

At ref. 874306, a path commences between two cottages and continues by a stone wall NNW across two fields to meet a farm road, which is then followed eastwards until the large Foxstones Farm is reached. A well-trodden path then leads down to the River Brun (marked as Brock Water on 1;25000 maps). The tree-lined river is crossed via a large,

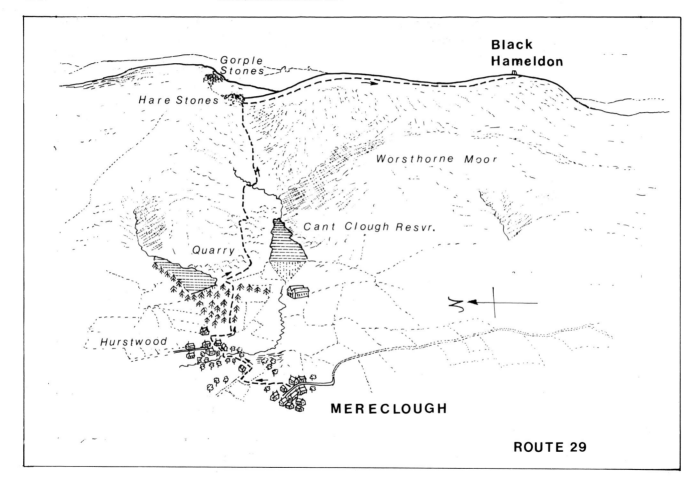

Gorple Stones

Black Hameldon

Hare Stones

Worsthorne Moor

Cant Clough Resvr.

Quarry

Hurstwood

MERECLOUGH

ROUTE 29

sturdy stone bridge and a narrow path then climbs to the sleepy parish of Hurstwood, once the home of the celebrated sixteenth century poet, Edmund Spenser, whose works include "The Faerie Queen". Hurstwood Hall, in the village centre, dates from 1579.

Beyond the hall, the route continues along the road to Hurstwood Reservoir, which passes through an avenue of pine and rhododendron before reaching the water's southern shores. From here an old cart track continues eastwards through disused quarry workings which extend to the northern banks of the Cant Clough Reservoir. This lake lies under the vast grassy flanks of Worsthorne Moor, whose monotony is relieved by the rent carved out by Black Clough. From the termination of the quarry track, a path then climbs E.N.E. towards the col between Gorple Stones (N) and Black Hameldon (S). Here the gritstone outcrops known as Hare Stones are clearly discernible on the skyline and can act as a guide, providing atmospheric conditions allow. In the upper reaches the terrain is tougher and the sketchy path passes through tussocky grassland and then, beyond a stream crossing (Rams Clough) at ref. 908315, a reed-covered marshy area.

The col is a good place to dwell for refreshments, for the Hare Stones always provide a good shelter from the prevailing wind. (Hoof Stones Height has no shelter) The huge rocks are also a good viewpoint and new vistas to the east, across the wild hollow housing the Gorple Reservoirs, can then be studied in relative comfort.

From Hare Stones, the path climbs on Black Hameldon's firm, peat-scarred slopes to gain the long broad ridge which spans just over a mile to the summit, Hoof Stones Height. Unfortunately the broadness of the ridge restricts views of the Calder Valley, but the airy situation and wide views of the hills of Derbyshire, West Lancashire and the Craven Hills more than compensate.

Alternative return routes include descending south to the Long Causeway (metalled road), which leads directly back to Mereclough - a distance of 3½ miles. Also possible is a north-western descent across the rugged Black Clough, joining the main route north of Cant Clough Reservoir.

ROUTE 30
BLACK HAMELDON from Todmorden

Distance 6 miles (one way) - moderate to hard

This is the longest ascent to Black Hameldon but those who undertake it will be rewarded by its intricate and changing moods.

A wide path, zig-zagging on the steep slopes out of the busy Calder Valley, commences at Lobb Mill Picnic Site (ref. 956247), which lies close to the railway viaduct. The railway disappears through a tunnel beyond the viaduct and thus its crossing becomes unnecessary. Height is rapidly gained on the firm, tree and crag-lined track and the views of the Calder Valley improve. Looking over the bracken-cloaked, declining slopes to the valley, the gentle curves of the railway line, canal

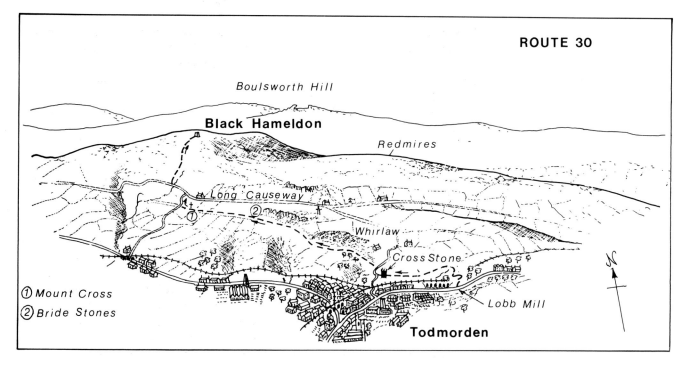

ROUTE 30

Boulsworth Hill

Black Hameldon

Redmires

Long Causeway

Whirlaw

Cross Stone

Lobb Mill

Todmorden

① Mount Cross
② Bride Stones

and the busy road all lead the eye to Todmorden, whose urban spread has been curtailed by the crowding hills. High above woodlands, stark mills and tall chimneys Stoodley Pike dominates northern scenes.

   After passing by some farm buildings, the route follows an old walled track westwards to a wooded ravine. The track is abandoned at ref. 956251, where the ravine is circum-vented on a shrub-lined path which can become muddy. This terminates at a country lane just west of Cross Stone. An old church, which will probably have been noticed in views from the valley, is then reached. What is surprising and a little sad, is that on close inspection, it is derelict - just a soot-stained shell. Apparently the church, rebuilt in 1835 has been sub-jected to landslip and will soon be demolished. This will please many of the locals who feel it is a monstrosity which does not belong amongst the existing quaint old cottages.

At a road junction, a right turn is taken before turning left on a track, which passes the golf course and some old quarries. The cragged pike of Whirlaw Stones crowns the skyline and the route continues towards this, before meeting the Calderdale Way amidst sylvan scenes above the verdant hollow of Hole Bottom.

The route actually passes to the south of Whirlaw Stones on the open fells of Whirlaw Common, but a detour can be made, if required. Across the common, the track becomes paved with smooth slabs of millstone grit. This was an ancient pack-horse road and, a few hundred years ago, would have been used to convey coal from Cliviger and lime from Clitheroe. It becomes enclosed once more to the south of the Bride Stones. It is well worth a detour to see these outcrops, for they are some of the weirdest gritstone boulders north of the Dark Peak! The track reaches the Shore Road at ref. 914274, close to the 7th century Celtic Mount Cross, which once marked a crossroads of ancient highways. The Shore Road then climbs northwards to reach the Long Causeway, a high lane linking Burnley with Hebden Bridge.

At ref. 913282, by a small stream, the lane is left and a northbound course across rough grass and peaty terrain leads to Hoof Stones Height, the summit at the southern end of the Black Hameldon ridge. The concrete trig point, is surrounded by shallow pools, except after periods of drought. Unfortunately the broadness of the ridge restricts views of the nearby Calder Valley but there is compensation in the form of extensive panoramas encompassing the peaks of Derbyshire, the Craven Hills, (notably Pen-y-Ghent) and Lancashire's noble escarpment, Pendle Hill.

ROUTE 31
BLACK HAMELDON from the Widdop Reservoir

Distance 4 miles (one way) - moderate to hard

The best eastern approach to Black Hameldon commences from the Widdop Reservoir, which lies to the south east of Nelson in a deep basin between the crag-interspersed, grassy slopes of Widdop Moor and Flask.

After crossing the causeway along the top of the large earth-fill dam (ref.936328), the route follows a rough track by the reservoir's southern shores. High on flanks above, the dark mysterious crags of Cludders Slack offer, to those with imagination, endless permutations of figures and faces, sculpted from northern grits. Beyond a small conifer copse, the track climbs steep, grassy hillsides and, at ref. 927325, meets another path before zig-zagging to the airy slopes of Black Moor. Here the Gorple Lower Reservoir first comes into view. In retrospective views across the hollow of Widdop, the distinctive protuberances of Dove Stones and near neighbour Boulsworth Hill dominate the skyline.

The path, an ancient road known as the Gorple Gate Track, is sketchy hereabouts, but its grassy groove can be followed for a while. It becomes obvious once more on reaching the edge of a wide, wild basin from where the Gorple

Black Hameldon and the Gorple Upper Reservoir from Shuttleworth Moor

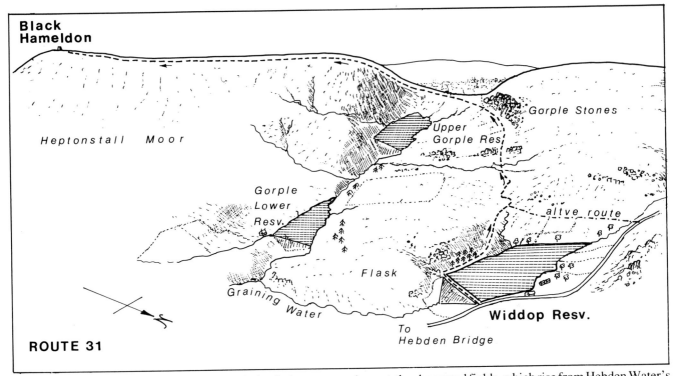

ROUTE 31

Upper Reservoir is revealed, basking beneath the dark, peaty slopes of Black Hameldon. A line of angular gritstone slabs descend from the path to the reservoir's shores. Beyond the spread of the barren Heptonstall Moors is Stoodley Pike, whose famous monument stands prominent in a hillscape which recedes to the pale blue Derbyshire Peaks. In views to the east, the chequered fields, which rise from Hebden Water's valley, contrast pleasingly with the surrounding moorland scenery.

Further west, the gritty track passes the Gorple Stones, where steep slopes are interspersed with crags and boulders. At ref. 914321, on the western edge of the crags, the track is left for a path which indistinctly crosses an area of cotton-grass cloaked marshland. It becomes clearer on reaching firmer ground and passes the Hare Stones, which guard a col between the Gorple Stones and Black Hameldon. At this point new landscapes unfold. Pendle Hill rises, ever dominant above the industrial East Lancashire plains. In western views, the moorlands descend to Cant Clough Reservoir, from whose southern shores rise the rippled flanks of Worsthorne Moor and, in the middle distance across the depression of the Cliviger Gorge, are the crinkle-cut cliffs of Thieveley Scout.

The path then continues southwards climbing Black Hameldon's slopes on a route previously described from Mereclough.

Although it would add an extra six miles to the journey (making fourteen in all), a possible return route for intrepid travellers would be to descend southwards from the summit to the Long Causeway road where an eastbound course past Blackshaw Head to ref.967275 would lead to the Pennine Way route. This could then be followed down to Colden Water, before traversing Heptonstall Moor to the Gorple Lower Reservoir and meeting the Nelson to Hebden Bridge road at ref.949319, a mile from the Widdop Reservoir's dam and very close to the Pack-Horse Public House (ref. 952317).

Gorple Stones

WOLF STONES

> O.S. Landranger Map (1:50000) No. 103
> Pathfinder (1;25000) SD83/93 (route 33) SD84/94 (32)
> Outdoor Leisure Map (1:25000) No. 21 'South Pennines' (from Ponden)
>
> Route 32 From Glusburn
> Route 33 From the Ponden Reservoir, Worth Valley

When travelling on the Colne to Haworth road in the region of the Water Sheddles Reservoir, prominent rock outcrops can be seen on the northern skyline above bare moors. They are known as the Great Wolf Stones and, along with the Little Wolf Stones and a concrete trig. point, crown the summit of the Ickornshaw and Keighley Moors. These are the most northerly outliers of the hills defined as the Southern Pennines.

The higher slopes are dark, peaty and covered profusely with heather - really tough hill-walking country! They cannot, unfortunately, be explored at will, for they are the domain of the grouse shooters. Evidence of these predators' presence can be seen regularly, especially on Ickornshaw Moor where there are numerous shooters' huts and grouse butts. The northern slopes of Ickornshaw Moor decline to the farm-lands that surround the River Laneshaw and Lumb Gill Beck. The latter flows by the villages of Cowling, and Ick-ornshaw - isolated pockets of industry interrupting an otherwise pastoral landscape.

Wolf Stones has its own lake, albeit a modest man-made affair. The Keighley Moor Reservoir lies to the west of the summit in a moorland combe high above the attractive vale of Newsholme Dean. Beyond here, the western flanks merge tamely with the Aire Valley at the busy weaving town of Keighley.

To the south of the hill is the lovely Worth Valley, where the Ponden Reservoir basks in a scene as green and pleasant as any in the Emerald Isles. If the eye follows the valley westwards, there is a stark contrast, for the Water Sheddles Reservoir lies on a wild and lonely moorland pass where the colours become muted- ochre dappled with sombre russets and umber. Here too lies a strange beauty - the epitome of the harsh and dramatic auras created and illustrated by the pen of Emily Brontë in 'Wuthering Heights'. These hills were amongst the countryside that the Brontë sisters knew and loved so well.

ROUTE 32
WOLF STONES from the Dog and Gun Inn, Glusburn

Distance 5 miles (one way) - moderate to hard

This is by far the finest route to the summit of Wolf Stones and passes though a variety of diverse scenery. It starts

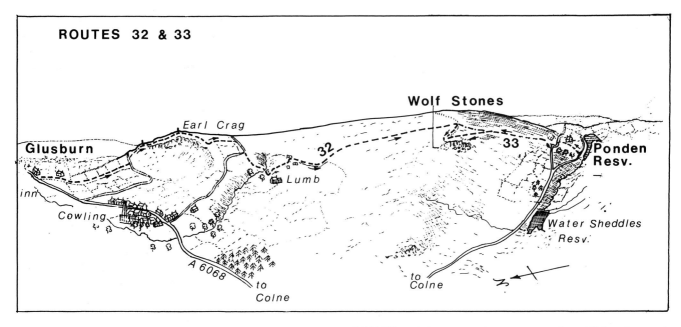

at the A6068 road at ref. 993444, to the west of the old stone-built 'Dog and Gun Inn'. A track is followed southwards past High Malsis Farm. In views ahead across lush meadows, the high moors are obscured by a steep hill, Earl Crag capped by gritstone outcrops and adorned with two curious monuments - to the east, the castellated Lund's Tower and to the west, Wainman's Pinnacle.

Beyond High Malsis, the path follows a dry-stone wall on its right hand side, traversing fields to Brush Farm (ref. 989433) and thence south to a country lane. This rakes to the eastern extremities of Earl Crag where it is is abandoned for a track, which climbs to Lund's Tower. The monument is seen at close quarters to contain a spiral staircase, leading to a viewing tower. The views really are quite spectacular from here! Emerald Airedale is laid before you with the distant towns of Keighley and Skipton, lying snug beneath Rombalds and Embsay Moors. To their north are the pale Craven Hills, those southern outliers of the Yorkshire Dales. In the west, guarded by that other sentinel, Wainman's Pinnacle and in the valley of Lumb Gill Beck, lies the village of Cowling.

On leaving Lund's Tower, a delightful promenade follows, tracing the cliff's edge to Wainman's Pinnacle, built on a huge gritstone outcrop. Cowling can now be seen more intimately. Its splendid parish church and tall mill chimney

Wainman's Pinnacle

stand prominent amongst terraces which huddle beneath the rolling green pastures that rise to Cowling Hill. These airy scenes contrast with the ones to the south for here the dark Ickornshaw Moor rises starkly to the horizon with little to entice the walker to continue beyond this present honey-pot. DO continue however, there are rewards!

At the western edge of Earl Crag, a track leads southwards to reach Piper Lane at ref. 983425. The lane is then followed until it bends sharply northwards towards Cowling. At this point it is abandoned for a walled track (Close Lane) which continues westwards into the splendidly silky landscapes of Lumb Head, where small deciduous woodland, pasture and stream are tightly enclosed by a steep-sided glen. The path descends to a tributary of Lumb Head Gill before crossing the main stream and climbing westwards to join the Pennine Way route at a walled farm track (ref. 965421). After passing through a gate at the end of the track, the route circumvents Lumb Head where there are views of a waterfall, which must have been pleasant once upon a time (Wainwright deemed it enough of a highlight to illustrate in his P.W. Companion). To me it is an example of how man needlessly damages his environment. Close to the point where it cascades into a sylvan hollow, the beck has been spanned by two tasteless squared arches under a bridge which conveys the path. When I last visited the scene, coloured empty fertilizer bags and other such rubbish littered the stream and, at the base of the falls were a couple of discarded car tyres! More pleasant views across Lumb Head reveal Earl Crag, which appears,

The Great Wolf Stones

from this vantage, as a conical hill, crowned solely by Wainman's Pinnacle. This is the focal point in a gentle landscape where hillslopes are accentuated by the pattern of field boundaries and decorated by copses and dark stone farmhouses.

The route from here is complex but, being well waymarked, is fairly easy to follow. Beyond the waterfall, a path rises south-eastwards across rough pastures and eventually reaches a group of ruined farm buildings (ref. 970418). It then descends briefly to a stream, Andrew Gutter, which flows between them. After climbing to the most easterly ruin, situated by a wall corner, the path changes direction, going through a gate and following the wall southwards until three shooters' huts are reached. From here there are two possible routes. The first is the Pennine Way route where an intermittently sketchy path continues southwards over the rough heathery terrain of Ickornshaw Moor. A more used alternative (marked by a broken black line on 1:50000 O.S. maps) continues past the huts and climbs south westwards on an obvious track to a lone hut. A well cairned track then rejoins the Pennine Way route at the 400 metre contour. Cairns continue to highlight the way to the ridge where a well-defined track goes south westwards, parallel to the fence, to reach the summit.

As one stands on the Great Wolf Stones, the wide southern panoramas are seen for the first time. The dominant peaks in these views are Boulsworth Hill, rising from the wild pass which cradles the lonely Water Sheddles Reservoir and, further distant across the industrial East Lancashire PLains, the escarpment of Pendle Hill. To the south east, the beautiful Worth Valley snakes to the distant village of Haworth.

A suitable variation on the return journey would be to follow the Pennine Way to Cowling. This would mean retracing steps to the Lumb Head Waterfall and then continuing southwards to the village. A path which follows Lumb Mill Beck(not named on 1;50000 maps) and running parallel to the A6068 road,could then be followed to reach a country lane at ref. 982444. This lane then joins the main road just to the west of the starting point at 'The Dog and Gun Inn' where sustenance would be well deserved!

ROUTE 33
WOLF STONES from the Ponden Reservoir

Distance- 2 miles (one way) - moderate (steep initial climb)

This is the shortest legal route available to the summit. (the most direct from Water Sheddles Reservoir, although over open moorland, is not sanctioned by its owners, the Water Authorities.)

The path, which begins by the Ponden Reservoir in the Worth Valley (ref. 986376), is the one used by Pennine Way travellers until we deviate on the final stretch to the summit. Its initial ascent across the farmlands of the Dean Fields is very steep, and probably the most demanding section of the route. The going becomes easier as the Dean Clough Woods are entered, prior to reaching the high, winding Oakworth Lane, which is followed around the head of the clough past some rustic stone terraced cottages. When I was last here it was springtime and the place was enhanced by splashes of colour provided by daffodils and the new chrome green foliage of trees and shrubs. There are lovely views southwards to the lush Worth Valley and the cavernous, wild ravine of Ponden Clough, the most spectacular feature of the moors beyond.

At ref. 985378, the lane is left for a stony track which climbs past an unsightly and badly placed rubbish tip. A reedy path guided by a tall dry-stone wall is then utilised to climb north-westwards over moors of rough grass, interspersed with clumps of heather and bilberry. The wall terminates on the curiously named Old Bess Hill and soon the squarish profile of the Great Wolf Stones comes into view on the western edge of the moor. On the shoulder of the stones is Boulsworth Hill, whose angular profile, being more shapely than its surrounding satellites, commands attention, especially as height is gained and panoramas widen. The brow of Old Bess is reached

and a cairned track traverses a marshy area of heather-cloaked peat. Duck-boards are strategically placed over the worst spots and therefore, even after rainy periods, there is little difficulty in negotiating a safe passage.

At Bare Hill, the path veers to the east of Wolf Stones and a beeline can be made across rough tussocky grasslands. In my opinion, however it is better to follow the main path to a point a few yards beyond the ridge fence. Here a shooters' track leading westwards offers an effortless stroll along the heathery ridge to the summit, where the concrete trig. point is elevated on a grassy mound surrounded by gritstone boulders. The Great Wolf Stones lie just to their west beyond the fence. After passing through the bare and featureless landscapes of the hill's southern slopes, the northern vistas across the rolling hills of Lothersdale and the fertile Aire Valley to the famous Three Peaks of Yorkshire are a revelation - a pleasing contrast, and one that makes this short walk worthwhile.

On the summit of Wolf Stones